Global Health

Published in 2026 by Scientific American Educational Publishing
in association with **The Rosen Publishing Group**
2544 Clinton Street, Buffalo NY 14224

Contains material from Scientific American®, a division of Springer Nature America, Inc.,
reprinted by permission, as well as original material from The Rosen Publishing Group®.

First Edition

Scientific American
Lisa Pallatroni: Project Editor

Rosen Publishing
Oli Wiggins: Compiling Editor
Michael Moy: Senior Graphic Designer

Cataloging-in-Publication Data

Names: Scientific American, Inc.
Title: Global health / edited by the Scientific American Editors.
Description: Buffalo, New York : Scientific American Educational Publishing, an imprint of Rosen
Publishing, 2026. | Series: Scientific American explores big ideas | Includes glossary and index.
Identifiers: ISBN 9781538313015 (pbk.) | ISBN 9781538313022 (library bound)
| ISBN 9781538313039 (ebook) Subjects: LCSH: Public health–International
cooperation–Juvenile literature. | World health–Juvenile literature.
Classification: LCC RA441.G563 2026 | DDC 362.1–dc23

Manufactured in the United States of America
Websites listed were live at the time of publication.

Cover: PeopleImages/istockphoto.com

CPSIA Compliance Information: Batch # CSSA26.
For Further Information contact Rosen Publishing at 1-800-237-9932.

CONTENTS

INTRODUCTION

The health of the global population and the planet itself has been a priority for a functioning society since the world began. Over the years, researchers and scientists have dedicated their lives to studying viruses, nutrition, mental health, and more.

Viruses, such as COVID-19, have given researchers a look into how pandemics work in a modern age, from first infection to when a pandemic is really over. Researchers also delved into how events like a pandemic have affected the mental health of people worldwide, and how to practice moments of self care and wellbeing.

Scholars have also noticed that the world itself is in some sort of a health decline. With climate change at an all time high, natural disasters such as wildfires have become more deadly. Journalists and scientists have been studying the ways in which this impact on the planet is affecting its inhabitants, from smoke inhalation to water pollution after hurricanes.

Historians have looked back at where our food quality standards began and nutritionists now study our food, diet, and exercise in order to get an idea as to what's best to eat, and what's better to eat in moderation.

With all this information on what is causing global health to decline, it's important to learn how to care for oneself, too. Articles have come out on how exactly to cope, survive, and thrive in this ever changing world. In this edition of *Scientific American*, such topics will be explored in hopes of giving a better understanding of the health of the world at large.

Section 1: COVID19 and Pandemic Response

Why Some People Get Sick More Often

By Elana Spivack

Everyone gets sick. Despite all the vegetables we eat or vitamins we gulp down, sooner or later pathogens such as viruses and harmful bacteria infiltrate our bodies, and we need to take a time-out. We sit back and let our immune system do its job.

But when it comes to getting sick, not all immune systems are equal. Some people seem to get sick much more often than others. One could easily conclude that these individuals—such as elementary school teachers or hospital workers—are merely exposed to sick people more often. But susceptibility to illness isn't as simple as the odds of being exposed to someone with a cold. Each person gets sick differently.

Moreover, people recover differently. Not everyone returns to their baseline level of health after the flu or COVID. The biology behind why and how some people get sick more often than others is still largely unknown. But a paper published in 2023 in *Nature Communications* shines a light on the components of immune resilience—the ability to restore immune functions that stave off diseases and control inflammation caused by infectious diseases, as well as other sources of inflammation.

Scientific American spoke with the study's lead author, Sunil Ahuja, a professor of medicine at the University of Texas Health Science Center at San Antonio and director of the Department of Veterans Affairs Center for Personalized Medicine, about why some people fall ill more often.

[An edited transcript of the interview follows.]

Q: Why are some people more susceptible to getting sick?
A: In general, one would consider three main factors. One would be genetic susceptibility: you're born with a genetic predisposition to becoming infected more easily. You could have inborn errors,

such as polymorphisms in genes that are well described for host immunity.

Second would be environments where there's a heavy burden of infection. If you look at our ancestors, a lot of them passed away by the time they were in their 50s because they had a greater antigenic load [the amount of inflammatory stress an infection causes] before there were vaccines, higher living standards and better sanitation.

These are kind of static factors. But then the third factor is response to inflammatory stress. I might respond in one way to one infection and in another way to a different infection. It's a yin-yang. Environment plays a role, and that same genetic thing that's protective against one infection can be detrimental for another infection. People show variation in how they respond to these challenges—which could also have a genetic basis. When we respond to challenges, we all have what I would call "a burst of inflammation." We all need some inflammation, but it has to be the right amount at the right place at the right time. The injured or infected site gets swollen, red and warm. These signs of inflammation at that site are saying, "Help, I need white blood cells to show up at that site to ward off further spread of this inflammation and to allow for healing." The body produces these chemical substances, which we now call chemokines. "Chemo" stands for "chemoattractant"—it's the attractant for white blood cells.

There are people who can be hyperinflamed and hypoinflamed. People vary in their amount of inflammation. In our study, being able to control inflammation and preserve immunocompetence was associated with being asymptomatic. Some people are infected yet don't get sick, because they had a really good inflammatory response.

Q: It seems that people in some professions, such as teachers, get sick more often. Why is that?

A: One reason is in part related to the microbial load. You're taking 30 or 40 kids into close quarters. It's exposure. Not everyone will get sick. It's a subgroup of these people. This susceptibility is population-based, not individual-based. If I took a group of day care workers, they have so much exposure to respiratory viruses, influenza, and so on. The greater the exposure, the greater the likelihood there will be some degradation.

I told you about inflammation and how it can increase or decrease an effective immune response. We go through such cycles repeatedly in our life. There will be some people who, despite these repeated cycles, manage to preserve that resilience piece; there will be some people whose response is moderately degraded; and there will be some people who have this susceptibility at any age to degrade—that's what we call nonoptimal.

The traditional way of doing research is to compare the old versus the young. This presumes that the only thing that is different between a young person and an old person is their age when, in fact, that's not quite true. One might need to break down the old group into varying degrees of immune health. That'd be like saying, "I'm in my 60s" which I am—"and I'm now an old fart, and I'm like every other old fart." That may not be true. There are old farts who are 110 years old who do just fine.

As a whole, a group may be at greater risk of getting infections, but that risk is largely localized to those people with eroded immune health. Among that group is a subset who are susceptible to degraded immune resilience—that is, among people of a similar age. We know that as one grows older, one's immunocompetence declines. So these infections tend to degrade our immune health at any age.

Q: How can immune resilience affect a person's longevity?

A: We could categorize people into four groups. People who have high immunocompetence and low inflammation—by definition the most protected group—live longer. Then you have those with low immunocompetence and high inflammation. These people will, unfortunately, after controlling for age, die sooner than others. Those who have high immunocompetence, which is good, coupled with high inflammation, which is bad, have an intermediate lifespan. So do those who have low immunocompetence and low inflammation.

I want to give you an example of those cycles, such as in people who have had a natural influenza infection. Temporarily, they turned on so-called mortality-associated biomarkers. Over time there was a recovery process. We have these injury-repair cycles. If people have too much injury and not enough repair, they will have some residual inflammation. They got hit with influenza, and then, over time, they recovered, but there was a small group who had this residual stuff left behind.

Q: Are there ways to prevent an infection from seriously harming you?

A: That would be analogous to saying, "Can I be certain that when I go to my grocery store, some idiot does not want to kill me?" So I don't think so. Some of the fittest people have gotten the flu and passed away. Among people who have good immune health, can I predict a priori that they will do as well during an infection? I cannot predict that. That is the problem. We do know that people, even young people, who have poor immune health don't do so well after a vaccine. I could advise them that there is a chance that they may not do so well after getting vaccinated because of their immune health score.

I can only tell you ways to possibly prevent exposure risks that could potentially protect you.

Q: How can you reduce your risk of getting exposed to pathogens?

A: I'm still very pleased when I see older veterans walking into the hospital with a mask on because it tells me they still understand the basic principle that their immune health is poor, or they've been informed of it, and they protect themselves.

Your diet and, I suspect, most important, exercise also play a role. I suspect that people who maintain regular sustained exercise, not just periodic exercise, are afforded immune benefits. There's a huge behavioral component to all of this—to change human behavior to mitigate risk. I think behavioral change is so difficult.

The two major things that I would focus on are to use commonsense precautions and to address behavioral issues.

About the Author

Elana Spivack is a science journalist in New York City who covers reproductive health, food science, and more. Follow her on X @ElanaSpivack.

Confronting the Dangers of Silent Spread Is Necessary to Prevent Future Pandemics

By Joshua S. Weitz

The telltale runny nose of a common cold, or the fever and aches associated with the flu, mark the way we classify respiratory illnesses—with their symptoms. Public health messaging relies on these symptoms, urging those who are symptomatic to stay home and avoid others. That makes sense. It reduces the risk that one case becomes many.

But what if transmission is not necessarily linked to symptoms? COVID has shown that diseases can lead to catastrophic societal harm when they spread without symptoms. Hence, preventing future pandemics requires greater investment in targeted public health interventions to reduce transmission—including from infected individuals who feel fine.

Indeed, asymptomatic transmission was essential to COVID's transition from a fast-moving outbreak in Wuhan, China, in early 2020 into a global pandemic that led to more than one million reported fatalities in the U.S. by May of 2022. People who felt fine transmitted their infection to others before developing symptoms (during a presymptomatic phase) or even if they never developed symptoms. Comparisons of early outbreak data revealed that approximately half of infected individuals were asymptomatic. That would be good news if asymptomatic infections were nontransmissible. But that wasn't the case.

On February 23, 2020, researchers from China, France and the U.S. released a joint analysis of more than 450 COVID transmission events in 93 cities in China. The analysis focused on the serial interval: the time between when someone exhibits symptoms and when the person they infect exhibits symptoms. Counter to expectations, the analysis showed that COVID's serial intervals were often less than zero, meaning individuals exhibited symptoms before the person that infected them. These statistics were evidence of rampant presymptomatic transmission. Public health experts tried to raise the alarm that efforts to stop transmission via symptom screening (e.g., testing for elevated temperature or shortness of breath) were bound to fail and that "unprecedented measures" were needed to fight back.

The deadly consequences of asymptomatic transmission soon arrived in the U.S. On March 10, 2020, the Skagit Valley Chorale gathered outside Seattle for a rehearsal. Despite efforts to limit physical contact, within a few days it was evident that someone in the group had unwittingly infected others. Ultimately, 53 of the 61 attendees were infected, and two died. This superspreading event revealed that COVID could spread in the air in the absence of symptoms. Yet the relevance of asymptomatic transmission remained contested. On June 8, 2020, a top WHO official declared that asymptomatic transmission was "very rare." The pandemic was raging, but we were losing precious time to confront silent spread. The consequences were grave. As head of the White House Coronavirus Task Force, Anthony Fauci noted in August 2020: "I've never seen a viral disease in which you have such a wide breadth of symptoms, ranging from no symptoms at all, in 40–45 percent of cases, to severe enough to kill you." Asymptomatic transmission represents a double-edged sword. Individual outcomes may be better, but silent spread leads to many more infections that can lead to worse outcomes for the population.

What can be done to reduce asymptomatic transmission? Initial responses to the pandemic involved limitations on gatherings and stay-at-home orders. But COVID's unusual mix of severe and asymptomatic outcomes catalyzed a diverse group of stakeholders to invest in unconventional approaches to reduce the risk of silent spread. These approaches include real-time risk assessment, large-scale rapid testing, context-specific masking and improved indoor air quality. Each of these has a complementary role in reducing silent spread, and if implemented at scale, they can be essential weapons in the ongoing fight against pathogens of pandemic potential.

In the absence of symptoms, real-time risk assessment powered by outbreak models and disseminated via mobile-accessible dashboards could function as a threat forecast. These dashboards could provide mapped information on a variety of infectious disease risks, including upsurges of COVID reported in wastewater. People could then decide to avoid events whose risk exceeded their tolerance. However, even if someone attends an event, the use of on-site rapid testing and masks could limit infections. This could be an enormous force for good, especially in nursing homes and long-term care facilities, which had a disproportionately large fraction of overall COVID fatalities. Irrespective of individual action-taking, infrastructure investments in indoor air quality (via improved filtering, air turnover rates and upper room UV-C sterilization) could improve health outcomes.

Finally, we must commit significant resources to the development and effective dissemination of vaccines both in the U.S. and globally—especially in developing countries. The production of billions of doses of vaccines just a year after COVID's emergence represents an incredible validation of the power of basic research and public-private partnerships. However, producing vaccines does not always translate to getting shots into arms. Public health agencies must improve messaging to explain both why individuals can benefit from vaccines, when they should get vaccines (and boosters) and what each vaccine is meant to do. In the case of COVID, mRNA vaccines were shown to reduce rates of symptomatic illness by more than 90 percent. Yet these vaccines do not prevent all infections. This means vaccinated individuals can still get infected, test positive and infect others—but their risk of severe outcomes decreases. This is precisely the point. But the fact that vaccines did not provide perfect protection against infection (asymptomatic or otherwise) has accelerated the rampant spread of misinformation that threatens to diminish vaccine uptake—not just for influenza and COVID but also for preventable childhood diseases, including measles.

Nearly five years have elapsed since early warning signs emerged of a novel coronavirus spreading in Wuhan fueled by asymptomatic transmission that would soon lead to a global pandemic. At the time, the risk to public health and socioeconomic stability seemed far removed. Since then scientists, public health experts, government agencies and the biotech sector have developed a suite of countermeasures to confront the dangers of silent spread—yet there is more to do, including identifying the consequences of the silent spread of avian influenza in wild and domestic animals. Translating this momentum into data-driven threat assessments, high-impact interventions (spanning testing and air quality improvements), faster vaccine deployments and more effective messaging from doctors and public health agencies is essential to reduce the ongoing burden of COVID; these actions will better prepare the world to identify, prevent and respond to threats of pandemics to come—before it is too late.

This is an opinion and analysis article, and the views expressed by the author or authors are not necessarily those of Scientific American.

About the Author
Joshua S. Weitz is a professor of biology at the University of Maryland where he holds the Clark Leadership Chair in Data Analytics and an appointment at the University of Maryland Institute for Health Computing. Weitz is the author of multiple books including Asymptomatic: The Silent Spread of COVID-19 and the Future of Pandemics, *published by Johns Hopkins University Press in October 2024.*

How Risky Are Repeat COVID Infections? What We Know So Far

By Meghan Bartles

T he specter of COVID has haunted the globe for four years now—the disease has killed at least seven million people worldwide. Yet the pandemic's long-term effects are still hazy—because when it comes to a novel virus such as SARS-CoV-2, which causes COVID, scientists still have a lot to learn.

What we do know is that COVID is here to stay—and that catching it doesn't give people permanent immunity. Four years into the pandemic, researchers and clinicians know that people are racking up multiple infections, but the long-term consequences of repeatedly getting the virus aren't yet clear. Fortunately, both individuals and governments have strategies to avoid some infections—if they use them.

"However you slice it, whatever long-term health effect you look at, the risk [from reinfection] is not zero," says Ziyad Al-Aly, a clinical epidemiologist at Washington University in St. Louis. "The truth is that, yes, we're sick and tired of the virus, we're sick and tired of the pandemic—but it's still here. It's still hurting people."

In the U.S. alone, more than 1.1 million people have died of COVID since the pandemic began, according to the Centers for Disease Control and Prevention. The agency is no longer tracking infections at the community level, but in mid-January it reported that nearly four percent of deaths nationwide were caused by COVID.

And while the winter wave of infections appears to be waning, the world missed its chance to make COVID disappear. "This ugly guest isn't going to leave us any time soon," Al-Aly says. "It's going to be here probably for decades."

Early on in the pandemic, scientists hoped that COVID would be the sort of disease for which vaccination or infection creates immunity that lasts for years or a lifetime. But the SARS-CoV-2 virus had other plans. Vaccination and, to a lesser degree, infection make you less vulnerable to catching the virus and having a severe case, but that protection wanes over time.

"One infection does protect you against future infections" but not completely, says Jamie Rylance, a physician on the World Health Organization's clinical management team. The SARS-CoV-2 virus mutates rapidly, so a person's immune system can't necessarily fully fight off a new infection, even if it's been primed by a recent bout with a different strain. The same holds true for vaccinations: although initial shots and boosters help a person's immune system respond more effectively to an infection and reduce the odds of a serious COVID case, current COVID vaccines can't prevent infection completely.

Complicating things further, COVID often triggers asymptomatic infections, which helped the virus continue to spread early in the pandemic even in places where governments established relatively strict containment protocols. And four years into the pandemic, many people are testing for COVID less often and tests miss many asymptomatic cases, making them even harder to identify. So people have likely been infected more times than they know.

"We don't know how often we're getting reinfected because we have some protection from vaccination or even past infection," says Maria Van Kerkhove, interim director of the WHO's department of Epidemic and Pandemic Preparedness and Prevention. She doesn't think that's something to be complacent about, however. "We know that when the virus enters our body, it affects multiple organ systems," she says.

The combination of evidence on COVID and the long-term impacts of other viruses paints a grim picture of what it might mean to experience regular COVID infections.

"Every time you get infected [with COVID], it does harm to the body in some way," says Avindra Nath, a neurologist at the National Institutes of Health who has led research on long COVID and other postviral conditions. For example, a pulmonary infection can leave scars in the lungs or trigger blood clots. COVID may also interfere with the immune system itself, he says. Nath notes that the protective sheaths of many viruses include regions that can interfere with the immune system. Separately, one study that followed up with participants after a flu infection found that in about 30 percent of people, the immune system remained somewhat impaired two months later.

And because COVID is still relatively new, scientists realistically have no idea what happens 10, 20 or even 30 years after an infection, much less multiple bouts. "What we need to be able to track is the complications of pulmonary function [and] cardiac function five years from now, 10 years from now," Van Kerkhove says.

Frustratingly, we may never have a clear sense of the damage COVID reinfections are causing, says Sunil Ahuja, an infectious disease specialist at University of Texas Health Science Center at San Antonio. "To ascribe cause and effect is very challenging," he says of potential long-term consequences of repeated bouts with COVID. During the span of time between infections, "they've also had many other things happen to them, too."

Some viruses can hide out in the body and emerge decades after the initial infection to cause new problems. The virus that causes chicken pox, for example, can trigger shingles many years later. And scientists have recently learned that infection with the common Epstein-Barr virus seriously increases the risk of a person developing the autoimmune disorder multiple sclerosis. "I don't think we've seen the end of this movie yet," Al-Aly says of SARS-CoV-2's long-term impacts.

Moreover, COVID has already shown its potential to cause lasting harm in the form of long COVID, which can include debilitating fatigue, breathing problems, difficulty thinking, digestive issues and a wide variety of other symptoms. As of mid-2023 long COVID impacted 11 percent of Americans reporting a previous infection—a notable decline from the previous year. Scientists are still working to determine what triggers long COVID, but it's clear that people can develop the condition after several infections, not just their first encounter with COVID.

"Each time that you have COVID, you have a chance of having post-COVID condition afterwards," Rylance says, though he adds that "it's still fairly unpredictable at an individual level."

While scientists desperately want more data to better understand the ways COVID could shape a person's health for years to come, the hints available now are worrying, experts say. "There's a major concern here that people who are getting repeated infections [could] have long-term consequences," Nath says. "And the data that is coming out suggests that possibility."

Although COVID is now endemic and widely circulating, people and societies can both work to minimize the odds of infection, Van Kerkhove and Al-Aly say. For individuals, getting vaccinated and masking in public and crowded spaces remain the most effective strategies for avoiding COVID or reducing the severity of an infection. Unfortunately, just one in five adults in the U.S. had gotten the updated 2023-2024 COVID vaccine as of mid-January, according to the CDC—even though initial analysis of the vaccines shows that they are about 50 percent effective against infections, including by the latest subvariant, known as JN.1. Testing for COVID when feeling unwell and using antiviral medications such as Paxlovid also remain vital tools for reducing disease risk.

WHO's Van Kerkhove says that government action is key, including ensuring that masks, vaccines, tests and treatments are available and affordable. But she also called on governments to take bolder steps such as strengthening ventilation requirements in buildings and supporting the development of better vaccines, including an oral or nasal vaccine that could more effectively prevent against COVID in the respiratory tract, where the virus enters a person's body. In addition, Al-Aly says, we need a longer-lasting vaccine that would offer meaningful protection for several years, so people would not need to get vaccinated every year.

"It's not beyond the might of U.S. medicine to really develop the technology and to deliver those solutions," Al-Aly says of such next-generation vaccines. He says the investment is particularly important now that we understand that COVID is not a problem we will dispense with quickly—and now that concerns are mounting about the damage of repeated infections.

"Those are going to be the long-term, sustainable solutions," Al-Aly says. "It isn't sustainable to ask people to mask for the next 100 years."

About the Author

Meghan Bartels is a science journalist based in New York City. She joined Scientific American *in 2023 and is now a senior news reporter there. Previously, she spent more than four years as a writer and editor at Space.com, as well as nearly a year as a science reporter at* Newsweek, *where she focused on space and Earth science. Her writing has also appeared in* Audubon, Nautilus, Astronomy *and* Smithsonian, *among other publications. She attended Georgetown University and earned a master's degree in journalism at New York University's Science, Health and Environmental Reporting Program.*

COVID Rates Are Rising Again. Why Does It Spread So Well in the Summer?

By Tanya Lewis

It's that time of year: a thick, oppressive heat blankets everything, people huddle inside air-conditioned homes, offices, shops and cafes for respite—and COVID is surging again.

Levels of SARS-CoV-2, the virus that causes COVID, have increased in wastewater samples across the U.S., with the biggest uptick in the West. The percentage of positive tests—though not a perfect metric because people aren't testing as much—has also increased, but hospitalizations have remained relatively low. Most viral respiratory infections, such as influenza, peak in the winter. But for the four years that SARS-CoV-2 has circled the globe, it has caused peaks not just in winter but every summer, too. The question is, why?

Possible reasons for the summer COVID peak are complex, but they fall into three main categories: characteristics of the virus itself, characteristics of its human hosts, and environmental factors.

SARS-CoV-2 continues to evolve new variants. One rises to the fore every six months or so, according to Peter Chin-Hong, a professor of medicine at the University of California, San Francisco, who specializes in infectious diseases. In recent weeks several new subvariants of the virus's Omicron variant have emerged as dominant—including the so-called "FLiRT" variants (such as KP.2 and KP.3), as well as a newer variant called LB.1. These variants may be slightly more transmissible or better at evading the immune system than previous ones, Chin-Hong says.

Human behavior and the environment are other likely drivers of summer surges. During the summer, many people gather for events, travel for vacations or simply spend more time inside to beat the heat. The Northern Hemisphere winter has a string of holiday gatherings that are perfect for spreading disease; likewise, "in the summer, it's Father's Day, graduation, Fourth of July and then summer travel," Chin-Hong says. "It's kind of a like a one-two-three punch."

"We know that nearly all [COVID] transmission happens indoors, in places with poor ventilation and/or poor filtration," says Joseph Allen, an associate professor at the Harvard T.H. Chan School of Public Health and director of the Harvard Healthy Buildings Program. "One hypothesis is that these building factors and human behavior are driving the summertime increases in cases." Although many offices or other large buildings have an HVAC system that can pull in fresh air from outside, many houses and apartment buildings with window-mounted air conditioners do not. Instead these ACs simply recirculate stale, virus-laden air inside a room.

Some studies have shown that humidity and temperature can also affect SARS-CoV-2 transmission. The virus is thought to survive best when humidity and temperature are low because cool and dry air holds less moisture—so virus-trapping microscopic droplets can remain airborne longer before settling on the ground. But these factors are probably less significant than human behavior and the characteristics of SARS-CoV-2 itself. Early in the pandemic, scientists thought summer might slow COVID because the virus is exposed to higher heat and more solar ultraviolet light." But look at Florida and tropical countries," Chin-Hong says. "There was no break."

It's a persistent mystery why COVID spreads so efficiently in the summer as well as winter, whereas flu tends to be mostly a winter disease, says Linsey Marr, a professor of civil and environmental engineering at Virginia Tech, who specializes in aerosol transmission of pathogens. "I've studied the seasonality of the flu for many years, and we have some hypotheses about why it peaks in the wintertime," Marr says. One is that the flu virus survives better in dry conditions. Another is that our immune system is weaker in winter, and a third is that heated buildings are tightly sealed and recirculate contaminated air. In the summer, some of these conditions apply in cool, air-conditioned buildings—yet we don't see a summer flu peak. SARS-CoV-2 appears to be hardier than the flu virus, Marr notes, so it might simply be able to survive conditions that flu can't.

With climate change bringing more frequent and severe heat waves to much of the U.S. and the world, people will likely be spending even more time indoors in summertime—and so will SARS-CoV-2. This year's summer surge appears to have started on the West Coast, which has already had several weeks of severe heat.

And then there's the human immune system. People's immunity to COVID may have waned since the last time they were vaccinated or infected in the fall or winter, making them more susceptible to getting sick. Fortunately, immunity from past exposure, in the form of memory T cells, keeps most people from getting severely ill. But waning antibodies mean people can still get infected.

Earlier this year the U.S. Centers for Disease Control and Prevention encouraged people aged 65 and older to receive a second booster of last fall's COVID vaccine. But fewer than a quarter of adults have even gotten a first booster since last fall. Chin-Hong recommends that if you haven't been vaccinated in the last year, you should do so now. Older adults—especially those who are immunocompromised, planning a trip or attending a large gathering such as a wedding—should consider a second booster, too. And the Food and Drug Administration recently authorized a new version of the vaccine for the fall that is targeted toward the FLiRT variant KP.2 or its predecessor, JN.1.

Of course, there are other steps people can take to avoid summertime COVID, and many of them will sound familiar: masking, breathing cleaner indoor air by increasing ventilation and filtration, and avoiding crowded indoor spaces.

Today, four years since COVID first emerged, most people have some level of immunity to SARS-CoV-2 through vaccination, infection or both. And the virus is not nearly as deadly as it once was (although it still poses a danger to chronically ill or immunocompromised people, and long COVID is always a risk). At this point, Allen says, we'd be better off finding more structural solutions, such as redesigning buildings to allow for both climate control *and* clean, healthy air, instead of having to choose between them. "We've been fed this false narrative that it's energy efficiency or healthy indoor air," Allen says. "I reject that. And everyone should reject that. We can have both."

About the Author

Tanya Lewis is a senior editor covering health and medicine at Scientific American. *She writes and edits stories for the website and print magazine on topics ranging from COVID to organ transplants. She also appears on* Scientific American's *podcast* Science, Quickly *and writes* Scientific American's *weekly Health & Biology newsletter. She has held a number of positions over her eight years at* Scientific American, *including health editor, assistant news editor and associate editor at* Scientific American Mind. *Previously, she has written for outlets that include* Insider, Wired, Science News, *and others. She has a degree in biomedical engineering from Brown University and one in science communication from the University of California, Santa Cruz. Follow her on Bluesky @tanyalewis. bsky.social.*

Long COVID Is Harming Too Many Kids

By Blake Murdoch

Since the COVID pandemic began, claims that the disease poses only minimal risk to children have spread widely, on the presumption that the lower rate of severe acute illness in kids tells the whole story. Notions that children are nearly immune to COVID and don't need to be vaccinated have pervaded.

These ideas are wrong. People making such claims ignore the accumulating risk of long COVID, the constellation of long-term health effects caused by infection, in children who may get infected once or twice a year. The condition may already have affected nearly six million kids in the U.S. Children need us to wake up to this serious threat. If we do, we can help our kids with a few straightforward and effective measures.

The spread of the mistaken idea that children have nothing to worry about has had some help from scientists. In 2023 the American Medical Association's pediatrics journal published a study–which has since been retracted–reporting the rate of long COVID symptoms in kids was "strikingly low" at only 0.4 percent. The results were widely publicized as feel-good news, and helped rationalize the status quo, where kids are repeatedly exposed to SARS-CoV-2 in under ventilated schools and parents believe they will suffer no serious harm.

In January 2024, however, two scientists published a letter with me explaining why that study was invalid. Some of the errors made it hard to understand how the study survived peer review. For example, the authors claimed to report on long COVID using the 2021 World Health Organization definition, but didn't properly account for the possibility of new onset and fluctuating or relapsing symptoms, even though that definition and the subsequently released 2023 pediatric one emphasize those attributes. Any child with four symptom-free weeks–even nonconsecutive ones–following confirmed infection was categorized by the study authors as not having long COVID.

In August, the authors of the study retracted it. They did not admit to the errors we raised. But they did admit to new errors, and said these mistakes meant they understated the rate of affected children.

And that rate, according to other research, is quite high. The American Medical Association's top journal, *JAMA*, in August published a key new study and editorial about pediatric long COVID. The editorial cites several robust analyses and concludes that, while uncertainty remains, long COVID symptoms appear to occur after about 10 percent to 20 percent of pediatric infections.

If you're keeping score, that's as many as 5.8 million affected children in the U.S.—so far. And we know studies and surveys of adults have found that repeat infections heighten the risk of long-term consequences.

The *JAMA* study comparing infected and uninfected children found that trouble with memory or focusing is the most common long COVID symptom in kids aged six to 11. Back, neck, stomach and head pain were the next most common symptoms. Other behavioral impacts included "fear about specific things" and refusal to go to school.

Adolescents aged 12 to 17 reported different leading symptoms. Change or loss in smell or taste was most common, followed by body pains, daytime tiredness, low energy, tiredness after walking and cognitive deficits. The study noted that symptoms "affected almost every organ system." In other words, these symptoms reflect real physiological trauma. For example, SARS-CoV-2 can cause or mediate cardiovascular, neurological and immunological harm, even increasing the relative risk of new onset pediatric diabetes when compared with other lesser infections.

Children in schools today are often described as struggling with emotional regulation, attention deficits and developmental problems. Adolescents have some of the worst standardized test scores in decades. Pandemic measures such as school closures—most of which were short-lived and occurred several years ago—have been blamed almost entirely for children's present-day behavioral and learning problems.

While it is clear these early pandemic disruptions negatively impacted many children, the unproven notion that "the cure was worse than the disease" has become dogma and sometimes involves reimagining history. For example, the Canadian Pediatric Society's most recent COVID vaccination guidance fails to even acknowledge the existence of pediatric long COVID, while stating without evidence in its preamble that children were more affected by pandemic disruptions in activities than direct viral effects. It's hard to imagine how this wording could encourage pediatricians and parents to vaccinate children against a disabling virus.

Consider also a small but widely publicized Bezos Family Foundation–funded study which unscientifically claimed accelerated cortical thinning, a type of brain restructuring that occurs over time, is caused by "lockdowns." The study design could not demonstrate cause and effect, however, but only correlation. Pediatric brain experts have critiqued the research, pointing out that "no supporting evidence" was provided for the claim cortical thinning is from social isolation, and that it isn't necessarily pathological. "Lockdowns" were neither defined nor controlled for in the study, which relied on 54 pandemic-era brains scans from different children than the prepandemic scans they were compared to—meaning there was no measurement of brain changes in specific individuals. The pandemic-era scans came from months when relevant CDC seroprevalence data estimate that the number of children with one or more infections rose from about one in five to around three in five. We might reasonably predict that many of the studied brain scans were therefore from children who recently had COVID.

It is understandably disturbing to entertain the idea that we might currently be recklessly allowing millions of children to be harmed by preventable disease. That may be part of why problematic studies such as these have gotten headlines. It is more disturbing, however, that almost no public attention has been given to infection itself as a potential cause of children's behavioural and learning problems.

This makes no sense. We know that COVID harms the brain. Neuroinflammation, brain shrinkage, disruption of the blood-brain barrier and more have been documented in adults, as have cognitive deficits. These deficits have been measured as equivalent to persistent decreased IQ scores, even for mild and resolved infections. Millions of people have, or have experienced, "brain fog." What, then, do we guess a child's COVID-induced "trouble with focusing or memory" might be?

When you put together the estimate that 10 to 20 percent of infected kids may experience long-term symptoms, that many of the most common symptoms affect cognition, energy levels and behavior, and that children are being periodically reinfected, you have a scientific rationale to partly explain children's widely reported behavioural and learning challenges.

We can do something to protect our kids. We can vaccinate them every season, which somewhat reduces the risk of long COVID. We can keep sick children home by passing laws that create paid sick leave and end attendance-based school funding. We can normalize rather than vilify the use of respirator masks that help prevent the spread of airborne diseases.

Finally, we can implement fantastic new engineered indoor air quality standards designed to greatly reduce the spread of germs. Clean indoor air should be expected as a right, like clean water. The cost of providing cleaner indoor air is low relative to the economic benefits, which even when conservatively modeled are in the tens of billions annually in the U.S. and more than ten times the costs. These costs are also small compared to the price children and their families would pay in suffering as a result of preventable long-term impairment.

By regulating, publicly reporting and periodically inspecting building air quality, similarly to how we oversee food safety in commercial kitchens, we can greatly reduce the spread of disease and reap huge benefits for everyone—especially children.

This is an opinion and analysis article, and the views expressed by the author or authors are not necessarily those of Scientific American.

About the Author

Blake Murdoch is a health policy academic, bioethicist, lawyer and science communicator at the University of Alberta's Health Law Institute. He studies online health misinformation and pandemic discourse, engages in active ethics oversight for ongoing scientific research, and assesses disconnects between scientific evidence, ethical principles and policy.

Vaccination Dramatically Lowers Long COVID Risk

By Shannon Hall

A t least 200 million people worldwide have struggled with long COVID: a slew of symptoms that can persist for months or even years after an infection with SARS-CoV-2, the virus that causes COVID. But research suggests that that number would likely be much higher if not for vaccines.

A growing consensus is emerging that receiving multiple doses of the COVID vaccine before an initial infection can dramatically reduce the risk of long-term symptoms. Although the studies disagree on the exact amount of protection, they show a clear trend: the more shots in your arm before your first bout with COVID, the less likely you are to get long COVID. One meta-analysis of 24 studies published in October, for example, found that people who'd had three doses of the COVID vaccine were 68.7 percent less likely to develop long COVID compared with those who were unvaccinated. "This is really impressive," says Alexandre Marra, a medical researcher at the Albert Einstein Israelite Hospital in Brazil and the lead author of the study. "Booster doses make a difference in long COVID."

It is also a welcome departure from earlier studies, which suggested that vaccines provided only a modest defense against long COVID. In 2022 Marra's team published a meta-analysis of six studies that found that a single dose of the COVID vaccine reduced the likelihood of long COVID by 30 percent. Now, that protection appears to be much greater.

A study published in November in the *BMJ* found that a single COVID vaccine dose reduced the risk of long COVID by 21 percent, two doses reduced it by 59 percent and three or more doses reduced it by 73 percent. Vaccine effectiveness clearly climbed with each successive dose. "I was surprised that we saw such a clear dose response," says Fredrik Nyberg, an epidemiologist at the

University of Gothenburg in Sweden and one of the co-authors of the study. "The more doses you had in your body before your first infection, the better." That lines up with the findings of several new studies, which similarly show this ladderlike benefit. Marra's October 2023 meta-analysis found that two doses reduced long COVID likelihood by 36.9 percent and three doses reduced it by 68.7 percent. And in a study published last year in the *Journal of the American Medical Association*, other researchers found that the prevalence of long COVID in health care workers dropped from 41.8 percent in unvaccinated participants to 30 percent in those with a single dose, 17.4 percent with two doses and 16 percent with three doses.

These studies were conducted in various countries with differing health care systems, demographics, COVID vaccination uptake and COVID prevalence. As such, Marra notes that the COVID vaccines' effectiveness against long COVID will vary and may not be generalizable to other settings. Still, the consistency of the studies' findings is telling—regardless of their settings, many studies agree that boosters provide potent protection against long COVID. Marra's recent meta-analysis, for example, showed that the prevalence of long COVID in the early years of the pandemic was consistently above 20 percent. Today rates of long COVID have dropped, likely thanks to increased immunity, milder variants and improved treatment. Yet there is still a sharp divide between unvaccinated and vaccinated people. The prevalence of long COVID is currently 11 percent among those who are unvaccinated and 5 percent among those who have had two or more doses of the vaccine. "It is a significant difference for those who are unwilling to take the risk," he says.

The question is why. It could be that these vaccines help prevent severe COVID itself, which is a risk factor for long COVID. But that does not appear to be the whole story—in part because the boosters have also been shown to shield people who had only a mild COVID infection. Unfortunately, the precise mechanisms at play are hard to disentangle because the cause of long COVID itself is still cloaked in mystery. One possibility is that the virus lingers in the body, hiding in various organs—such as the gut or brain—and causing chronic inflammation. Another is that long COVID is an autoimmune disease in which the immune response triggered by the initial infection wages an extended war against the body, causing symptoms long after the initial infection has been cleared.

For both scenarios, boosters give people the upper hand, argues Akiko Iwasaki, an immunologist at Yale University who is co-leading a clinical trial on long COVID. That is because boosters enhance antibodies—increasing both their numbers and their ability to bind to the virus—as well as T and B immune cells that help fight the virus. With both components, "people who take the booster shots have an improved ability to fight off infection," Iwasaki says. And that is key, allowing the booster to quash a growing infection before it spirals out of control. "The more you can prevent the replication and spread of the virus within the body, the less chance the virus has to seed a niche—to establish reservoirs or cause excessive inflammation that leads to autoimmunity," she says.

Although it will take time to pinpoint the exact reason behind vaccines' protective effect against long COVID, many medical experts are hopeful that the new studies will help counter the spread of misinformation and disinformation about the COVID immunizations that has contributed to vaccine hesitancy. But experts also note that while vaccines reduce the risk of long COVID, they do not eradicate it, and protection may wane over time. "Breakthrough infections can still occur, and the dynamic of the virus—including the emergence of new variants—add complexity to the situation," Marra says. As such, he notes that it's important to continue to follow public health guidelines to minimize the impact of COVID, including the risk of long-term symptoms.

About the Author

Shannon Hall is an award-winning freelance science journalist based in the Rocky Mountains. She specializes in writing about astronomy, geology and the environment.

Masks Work. Distorting Science to Dispute the Evidence Doesn't

By Matthew Oiver, Mark Ungrin & Joe Vipond

M asks work. Especially respirator-style N95 masks. Amid an ongoing pandemic and outbreaks of influenza and RSV caused by airborne viruses, arguing over the virus-blocking power of masks remains one of the COVID era's signature follies. Disconcertingly, despite decades of evidence of their efficacy, some of the disagreement comes from a few in the medical field itself, misusing science and endangering lives.

Most recently a Cochrane review, which systematically assesses multiple randomized controlled trials, provoked headlines after claiming a lack of evidence that masks prevent transmission of many respiratory viruses. Not for the public, health care workers, or anyone. "There is just no evidence that they make any difference," the lead author said in a media interview. This brought an unusual chastisement from the Cochrane Library's editor-in-chief, who stated it was "not an accurate representation of what the review found."

That wasn't the first time something like this has happened. Late last year, a randomized controlled trial claimed that N95 respirators were no better than medical (or surgical) masks for health care workers. Whereas scientists, engineers and occupational health and safety experts highlighted flaws (see its comments section) in the study, these two episodes point to a bigger fundamental question: whether these types of trials are suitable to test how well physical interventions like masks reduce viral transmission.

Medical assertions of exclusive "ownership" over the science of masks when they are used during a pandemic ignore the fact that they represent a well-understood engineered solution, with decades of widespread and successful use behind them. Demands to reject this evidence reflect a failure to recognize and respect interdisciplinary expertise that has undercut the global pandemic response.

Placing randomized trials above other types of research such as observational, lab and modeling studies, has interfered with the COVID response. A randomized trial approach that allows a few studies to cancel out a huge body of research from other disciplines has no basis in science.

Enthroning these trials atop medical decision-making started with the best of intentions. In the 1980s, experts wanted to better integrate scientific knowledge into medicine. Decisions then varied widely among practitioners based on disparate reading, experience and education. Refining medical decision-making to make it more repeatable, consistent and linked to evidence marked the laudable birth of the evidence-based medicine movement.

This effort included establishing a "hierarchy of evidence," the idea that some types of evidence are more useful to medical decision-makers than others. Expert opinion and observational studies are at the bottom of the pyramid, randomized trials in the middle, and at the top, systematic reviews of these trials, where researchers compile and review several clinical trial results to make broader, more conclusive statements as happens with Cochrane review.

Randomized trials underlie much of medical research, because the human body is messy. A chemical effective in a lab or an animal model might turn out useless, or even harmful, once inside a human body—or only in some people, depending on genetics, environment or underlying illness. Randomizing trial participants averages out that noise and reduces biases. By comparing treatment outcomes between randomly selected groups, we can hope to isolate effects, making these trials a "gold standard" in medical research. However, they often take time, many participants (especially if the expected differences are small) and big budgets. Even the most rigorous of trials can't tell you if a treatment would have been effective with a different protocol. For example, a trial of seat belts in airplane crashes couldn't say they work in cars.

Because these trials are so narrowly focused—and can disagree—systematic compilations and reviews such as those produced by the Cochrane organization can make medical decision-making quicker and easier. Relying on such reviews, of course, trades convenience over the rigor of digesting each study and gaining real knowledge; this is one concern with them.

For masks, are randomized trials an appropriate way of evaluating a basic engineered safety system in the first place? We don't rely on such trials for seat belts, bike helmets or life jackets, and the oft-cited randomized trial of parachutes is an old running joke. Why is that so hilarious? What do the engineers know that doctors don't?

In many scientific disciplines randomized trial methods are fundamentally inappropriate—akin to using a scalpel to mow a lawn. If something can be directly measured or accurately and precisely modeled, there is no need for complex, inefficient trials that put participants at risk. Engineering, perhaps the most "real-world" of disciplines, doesn't conduct randomized trials. Its necessary knowledge is well-understood. Everything from highways to ventilation systems—everything that moves us, cleans our air and our water, and puts satellites into orbit—succeeds without needing them. This includes many medical devices. When failures like a plane crash or catastrophic bridge collapse do occur, they are recognized and systematically analyzed to ensure they don't happen again. The contrast with the lack of attention paid to public health failures in this pandemic is stark.

"Does a mask protect me from aerosolized virus?" or "Does this seat belt keep me from flying through the window in an accident?" are different types of questions than "Does aspirin reduce death rates after a heart attack?" Imprisoning engineering and the natural sciences at the very bottom of an evidence hierarchy—at the same level as an expert opinion—is a mistake. As with seat belts, whether people use masks properly matters, but no randomized trial could conclude seat belts "don't work." At best, that type of trial would be a truly inefficient way to assess specific instructions and incentives to get people to use them properly.

A well-understood technology, respiratory protection has been validated over decades, with standards (NIOSH in the U.S., CSA in Canada) that codify protection from viruses and bacteria.

Mining, biomedical research, chemical processing, pharmaceutical production and many more industries follow these laws and standards worldwide. Without exaggeration, millions of people trust their lives to the effective "real-world" science of respirators, with no need for randomized trial evidence.

It is therefore deeply concerning that prominent medical figures have misrepresented the protection provided by masks, when the evidence supports N95 respirators or better, ideally with two-way masking.

Medical policy makers failed to learn the lesson of the 2003 SARS-1 outbreak, exposed again in the current global pandemic: a novel pathogen requires a precautionary approach that includes airborne respiratory protections until proven otherwise. With millions dead and immense—and still growing—personal and economic damage inflicted by long COVID, failing to adjust now will continue to do enormous harm.

It is not too late to do better.

This is an opinion and analysis article, and the views expressed by the author or authors are not necessarily those of Scientific American.

About the Authors

Matthew Oliver is an aerospace and electrical professional engineer, and citizen of the Métis Nation.

Mark Ungrin is an interdisciplinary biomedical researcher and an associate professor at the University of Calgary.

Joe Vipond is an emergency doctor in Calgary, Alberta, clinical assistant professor at the University of Calgary, the co-founder of Masks4Canada, and a member of the John Snow Project.

Section 2: Mental Health

COVID Is Driving a Children's Mental Health Emergency

By Julia Hotz

When COVID shut down life as usual in the spring of 2020, most physicians in the U.S. focused on the immediate physical dangers from the novel coronavirus. But soon pediatrician Nadine Burke Harris began thinking of COVID's longer-term emotional damage and those who would be especially vulnerable: children. "The pandemic is a massive stressor," explains Burke Harris, who is California's surgeon general. "Then you have kids at home from school, economic hardship, and folks not being able to socialize." These stresses could be particularly toxic for children, she and another state health official wrote to health providers in April 2020. Last week U.S. Surgeon General Vivek Murthy issued a similar warning about children for the entire country.

The toxicity has become all too real after 20 months, driven by not just disarray but death as well. As of this past June, more than 140,000 children lost a close caregiver—such as a parent—to COVID, according to research published in the journal *Pediatrics*. Since 2019 there has been a rise in suicide attempts among people younger than age 18, researchers at the Centers for Disease Control and Prevention found when they examined mental-health-related emergency room visits during the past three years. And a study of pediatric insurance claims filed between January and November 2020, conducted by the nonprofit FAIR Health, found a sharp increase in mental-health-related problems, especially generalized anxiety disorder, major depressive disorder and intentional self-harm. These and other distressing trends recently led the American Academy of Pediatrics and two other health organizations to declare that children's mental health is currently a national emergency.

Burke Harris says those patterns arise from what pediatric health specialists term adverse childhood experiences (ACEs). These events include 10 types of specific traumas that range from direct abuse and neglect to overall household dysfunction. The adverse experiences activate the brain's fight-or-flight system—a normal response to an immediate physical danger such as a bear rushing at you. But "what happens when the bear comes every night?" Burke Harris asks. Because adverse events put children in prolonged and repeated danger, it extends their stress response and creates damage.

When COVID disrupted the routine and resources that school and after-school care ordinarily provide, many children were left to face ongoing hazards at home, including parental issues such as intimate partner violence and substance misuse. Both of these problems significantly rose during the pandemic, according to researchers.

As the pandemic wore on, California, guided by Burke Harris's warnings, took some action to protect its children. This October the state legislature passed the ACEs Equity Act, a first-in-the-nation law requiring insurance that covers preventive care and pediatric services to also cover in-depth screenings for adverse events.And, since January 2020, California's ACES Aware initiative has been educating clinicians about nonmedical interventions available to patients facing adverse events, and the state's Medicaid program has paid eligible providers $29 per screening. Such regular screenings—which involve asking intimate questions in a nonthreatening and supportive manner—are linked to a variety of positive health outcomes. A recent literature review found patients associate these screenings with greater trust in their doctors. And clinicians say the screenings help them identify social factors that influence health, which allows them to offer more effective care.

Lisa Gantz, a pediatrician at the Los Angeles County Department of Health Services,is one of more than 20,000 health providers in California who have received free two-hour online training offered in the state. By teaching her how to screen for and respond to adverse events, Gantz says the training has changed the way she approaches clinical care. She remembers one recent appointment with an underweight four-month-old and his mother. "We had gone through all of the feeding [methods], and I really wasn't able to come up with a reason why this child wasn't growing," Gantz says. But when she talked to the mother gently about possible changes at home, Gantz learned the child's parents had recently separated. And the family faced newfound financial hardship—a circumstance true of nearly half of U.S. households by August 2020, according to a national survey.

"As soon as the mom felt safe, we learned that the husband was deported, finances were tighter, and the mom needed to water down her son's formula to make ends meet," Gantz says. "She was too embarrassed to tell me that before, plus a mom's not going to walk in for a checkup and say, 'By the way, dad's not here anymore.' But the screenings create a space to have these larger conversations about what's going on at home." With that information, Gantz was able to connect the mother and her baby with a social worker and to public services that could help them pay for more formula.

Gantz describes the work of treating adverse experiences as creating a "medical neighborhood"—a cohesive unit that responds to the multifaceted nature of children's mental health with equally multifaceted resources.

Efforts in other states are trying to reduce children's adversity by helping parents tackle their pandemic-related problems. In North Carolina, for example, the Raleigh-based nonprofit SAFEchild offers a Circle of Security Parenting (COSP) program. Small groups of parents in the program meet weekly to reflect on their behavior and improve their relationships with their children. Before teaching parents how to listen, the program first helps them feel heard.

That step is crucial if interventions are going to go beyond "telling people what to do" and actually create lasting change, says Ginger Espino, a COSP facilitator at SAFEchild. She notes that many parents in the groups are victims of adverse events in their own childhood. "It's about breaking that cycle of abuse and empowering parents to have confidence that they can meet any of their child's needs, even if those needs were not met during their own childhoods," Espino explains. By inviting participants to affirm their own strengths, talk about concerns, and construct what security looks and feels like within the safe support group, the program aims to help parents create that same loving, nurturing environment for children at home. "They realize, 'Oh, my child's not trying to drive me crazy. My child has a need, and I need to figure out how to meet that need,'" she says.

A few other states have recently introduced efforts to address the surge of pandemic-provoked adverse events. In May Maryland issued an executive order to create an ACE awareness day and announced a $25-million fund to expand the state's youth development programs to every county. And Wyoming is using California's approach to reimburse health providers for their ACE screenings of eligible Medicaid patients, says Elaine Chhean, who assists the executive director of the National Academy for State Health Policy, which co-published a paper on various ways that states try to prevent or mitigate adverse experiences.

Nationally, there have been a few moves to help deal with adverse events. In May bipartisan congressional representatives from Georgia and Utah introduced a bill to expand ACE research and data collection. And that month the nonprofit ACE Resource Network launched an awareness campaign called Number Story. The program, so named because a clinical questionnaire about adverse events gives a person a score based on the number of such experiences, uses conversations with celebrities such as John Legend and Camila Cabello to educate the public about adverse events and how to recognize when they are going through one or more.

Sarah Marikos, executive director of the ACE Resource Network, says such recognition can help change behavior and motivate people to seek help. "In my grandparents' day, it was the norm to smoke, but now it's not. And that's the same thing we want to do around ACEs," she says.

If you or someone you know is struggling or having thoughts of suicide, help is available. Call or text the 988 Suicide & Crisis Lifeline at 988 or use the online Lifeline Chat.

About the Author

Julia Hotz is a solutions-focused journalist with stories in the New York Times, Wired, Scientific American, *the* Boston Globe, Time *and more. She is the author of* The Connection Cure. *You can find her on Instagram and X at @hotzthoughts, and at www.socialprescribing.co.*

Social Media Can Harm Kids. Could New Regulations Help?

By Jesse Greenspan

This week Surgeon General Vivek H. Murthy released a warning about the risks that social media presents to the mental health of children and teenagers. Adolescent mental health has been declining for years, and an increasing amount of research suggests that social media platforms could be partially to blame. But experts continue to debate just how much impact they have—and whether new and proposed laws will actually improve the situation or will end up infringing on free speech without addressing the root of the problem.

Numerous studies demonstrate that adolescent rates of depression, anxiety, loneliness, self-harm and suicide have skyrocketed in the U.S. and elsewhere since around the time that smartphones and social media became ubiquitous. In fact, in the U.S., suicide is now the leading cause of death for people aged 13 to 14 and the second-leading cause of death for those aged 15 to 24. In October 2021 the American Academy of Pediatrics declared a "national state of emergency in children's mental health," stating that the COVID pandemic had intensified an already existing crisis. The U.S. Centers for Disease Control and Prevention issued a similar warning in 2022, after the agency found that nearly half of high school students reported feeling persistently "sad or hopeless" during the previous year. According to the CDC, LGBTQ and female teens appear to be suffering particularly poor mental health.

Yet the role social media plays has been widely debated. Some researchers, including Jean Twenge of San Diego State University and Jonathan Haidt of New York University, have sounded the alarm, arguing that social media provides the most plausible explanation for problems such as enhanced teen loneliness. Other researchers have been more muted. In 2019 Jeff Hancock, founding director of the Social Media Lab at Stanford University, and his colleagues completed a meta-analysis of 226 scientific papers dating back to 2006 (the year Facebook became available to the public). They concluded that social media use was associated with a slight increase in depression and anxiety but also commensurate improvements in feelings of belonging and connectedness.

"At that time, I thought of them as small effects that could balance each other out," Hancock says. Since then, however, additional studies have poured in—and he has grown a bit more concerned. Hancock still believes that, for most people most of the time, the effects of social media are minor. He says that sleep, diet, exercise and social support, on the whole, impact psychological health more than social media use. Nevertheless, he notes, social media can be "psychologically very detrimental" when it's used in negative ways—for instance, to cyberstalk former romantic partners. "You see this with a lot of other addictive behaviors like gambling, for example," Hancock says. "Many people can gamble, and it's not a problem. But for a certain subset, it's really problematic."

Some recent studies have attempted to clarify the link between social media and mental health, asking, for instance, whether social media use is causing depression or whether people are being more active on social media because they're depressed. In an attempt to present causal evidence, Massachusetts Institute of Technology economist Alexey Makarin and two of his colleagues compared the staggered rollout of Facebook across various U.S. colleges from 2004 to 2006 with mental health surveys taken by students at that time. Their study, published in 2022, found that swollen rates of depression and anxiety, as well as diminished academic performance, followed Facebook's arrival. Makarin says much of the harm they documented came from social comparisons: students viewed the online profiles of their peers and believed them to "[have] nicer lives, party more often, have more friends and look better than them." Facebook's parent company Meta did not respond to requests for comment by press time.

Other studies have obtained similar results. In one paper, participants were paid to deactivate Facebook for four weeks prior to the 2018 U.S. midterm elections and reported experiencing improved happiness and life satisfaction when they weren't on the platform. And in February 2023 researchers at Swansea University in Wales found likely physical health benefits, including a boost to the functioning of the immune system, when social media use was reduced by as little as 15 minutes per day.

"In total, there's a more and more coherent picture that, indeed, social media has a negative impact on mental health," Makarin says. "We are not saying that social media can explain 100 percent of the rise of mental health issues.... But it could potentially explain a sizeable portion."

Mitch Prinstein, chief science officer at the American Psychological Association (APA), which recently released recommendations for adolescent social media use, points out that there's nothing inherently harmful or beneficial about social media. "If I'm 12, and I'm reading *Scientific American* and going on social media to talk with my friends about how interesting the articles are," he says, then that's a far cry from "going on a site that's showing me how to cut myself and hide it from my parents." He suggests that social media companies should take down the potentially harmful content, letting youth use social media more safely.

In addition to toxic content, Prinstein worries about the effects of social media on young people's sleep—and therefore brain development. "No kid should be on their phone after 9 P.M.," he says, "unless they're going to sleep well into the morning." But actually closing down the social apps and putting that phone down is difficult, Prinstein says. This is in part because of the design of these platforms, which aim to hold users' attention for as long as possible. Kris Perry, executive director of the nonprofit Children and Screens: Institute of Digital Media and Child Development and a former senior adviser to California governor Gavin Newsom, agrees. Besides being sucked in by app design, she says, adolescents fear disappointing their peers. "Kids feel genuinely scared that they'll lose friendships, that they won't be popular, if they don't like their friends' posts instantly," Perry says.

The flood of new studies on social media's harms is spurring lawmakers to action. Except for the Children's Online Privacy Protection Act, which passed in 1998—years prior to the advent of smartphones or social media—the U.S. Congress has never really involved itself with what kids do online. "It's kind of the Wild West out there," Prinstein says of the lack of oversight. Since around 2021, however, when a Facebook whistleblower testified that the company knew its platforms harmed youth mental health—allegations that Facebook denied—both Republican and Democratic lawmakers have moved to follow Europe's lead on stronger Internet regulations. On the federal level, members of Congress have introduced a slew of overlapping bills: at least two would bar social media use outright for kids under a certain age, while others would restrict targeted advertising and data collection, give young users more control over their personal information, prioritize parental supervision, facilitate additional research and hold social media companies liable for toxic content viewed by minors. Though nothing has yet passed, President Joe Biden seems largely onboard with these measures. In his February State of the Union speech, Biden said, "We must finally hold social media companies accountable for the experiment they are running on our children for profit." And on the same day as the surgeon general's warning this week, the White House commissioned a task force to analyze how to improve the health, safety and privacy of kids who go online.

Meanwhile state legislatures have jumped into the fray. California recently passed a law designed to protect children's online data. Montana banned TikTok. And Arkansas and Utah mandated, among other things, that social media companies verify the ages of their users and that minors get parental consent to open an account. Similar bills are pending in many other states.

Of the federal bills currently pending, arguably the Kids Online Safety Act (KOSA) has gained the most attention thus far. Sponsored by Republican Senator Marsha Blackburn of Tennessee and Democratic Senator Richard Blumenthal of Connecticut, the bill would require social media companies to shield minors from content deemed dangerous. It also aims to safeguard personal information and rein in addictive product features such as endless scrolling and autoplaying. Supporters of KOSA include Children and Screens, the APA and the American Academy of Pediatrics, along with several parents whose kids died by suicide after being relentlessly cyberbullied.

On the opposing side, organizations that include the Electronic Frontier Foundation, a digital rights nonprofit, and the American Civil Liberties Union have come out against KOSA, stating that it might increase online surveillance and censorship. For instance, these parties have raised concerns that state attorneys general could weaponize the act to suppress content about, say, transgender health care or abortion. This is particularly problematic because it could negate some of the positive effects social media has on teen mental health.

Researchers acknowledge that social media can aid kids by, among other things, connecting them with like-minded people and facilitating emotional support. This appears to be especially important for "folks from underrepresented backgrounds," Prinstein says, "whether you're the only person around who looks like you or the only person with your identity in your family." If KOSA leads to the restriction of speech about LGBTQ issues, for instance, it could be detrimental to members of that community. "That support, and even accessing information, is a great benefit," Prinstein says. "There really was no other way to get that resource in the olden times."

Jason Kelley, associate director of digital strategy at the Electronic Frontier Foundation, says that rather than a bill like KOSA, he would prefer to see stronger antitrust laws that might, for example, increase competition among platforms, which could encourage each one to improve its user experience in order to win out. More options, he says, would force social media companies "to deal with the ways they ignore user interest and desire and safety and privacy."

As the debate continues over the best legislative fixes, essentially all the researchers Scientific American spoke to agree on one idea: more information about these platforms can help us figure out exactly how they're causing harms. To that end, KOSA would mandate that the social media companies open up their closely held datasets to academics and nonprofits. "There's a lot we don't know," Hancock says, "because we're prevented."

If you or someone you know is struggling or having thoughts of suicide, help is available. Call or text the 988 Suicide & Crisis Lifeline at 988 or use the online Lifeline Chat.

About the Author

Jesse Greenspan is a San Francisco Bay Area–based freelance journalist who writes about history and the environment.

Summertime Sadness Could Be a Type of Seasonal Affective Disorder

By Lauren Leffer

H as the heat got you down? You're probably not alone. Wintertime—with its long, dark nights—is the season most associated with low mood and depression. But sun-filled summer days can also bring on the doldrums, particularly for the subset of people who experience a summertime version of seasonal affective disorder (SAD)—a type of depression with a periodic pattern. Those with a lesser-known and lesser-studied summer SAD variant may feel "out of sync with the rest of the world" because they experience depression just as summer breaks and pool party invites pick up, says Thomas Wehr, a psychiatrist and scientist emeritus at the National Institutes of Health.

Depression can occur any time of year, but some research indicates that the warmer months can be particularly challenging for certain people. A growing number of studies indicate links between body temperature and depression, and high outside temperatures have been linked to mood and mental health crises. The prevalence of summertime SAD remains unclear, but as climate change makes extreme weather more common, understanding the effects of hot days on mental health—and developing new, effective treatments—has higher stakes.

What Is Summer SAD?

Wehr and his colleague Norman Rosenthal, a psychiatrist then at the NIH, coined the term SAD in the early 1980s based on their research into people with cyclical winter depression. After publication, they received some unexpected letters from people who vehemently attested to having the opposite condition: depression in the summer and improved mood in winter.

Wehr and Rosenthal's team investigated these accounts in a 1987 case report, which described 12 people who displayed a pattern of recurrent depressive episodes in the summertime. In a 1991 follow-up paper, they compared another 60 participants, half of whom seemed to have summer SAD and half of whom had winter SAD. Both groups met clinical criteria for depression that usually reoccurred seasonally, but the two cohorts experienced different symptoms.

Participants in the winter group "were very lethargic" and compared themselves to hibernating animals, says Rosenthal, who is now a professor at the Georgetown University School of Medicine. In contrast, the summer group was more "irritable" and "restless," he adds. The winter cohort more frequently slept, overate and experienced weight gain, whereas the summer cohort reported higher incidences of insomnia, reduced appetite and more frequent weight loss.

The prevalence of summer SAD "would be a complete guess" because of limited data, Rosenthal says. Based on his interactions with people who do have the condition, Wehr believes it may be more common in warmer and more humid locations and in regions with limited access to air-conditioning. But Rosenthal and Wehr say much more work is needed to truly understand how common summer SAD is and where it most frequently occurs.

Compared with the winter variant, "the literature on summer SAD is much smaller," says Kelly Rohan, a clinical psychologist who studies subtypes of recurrent depression at the University of Vermont. Both the 1987 and 1991 studies had a small sample size, and there has been minimal follow-up work. Nevertheless, Rohan says those early case studies are robust and convincing because they thoroughly examine and describe peoples' symptoms.

Much research has linked winter SAD to shorter daylight hours and reduced sunlight exposure, causing clinicians to suggest light therapy as a potential treatment. In contrast, Rohan says, the primary triggers for the summer type are assumed to be heat and humidity.

Some researchers question whether SAD—either the summer or winter variety—should be a medically recognized condition altogether. "As it's conceptualized, I am skeptical," says Steven Lobello, a psychology professor at Auburn University at Montgomery. In 2016 Lobello and his colleagues published a study involving survey data from 34,000 people in the U.S. that found no population-level indication that depressive episodes were more common in the winter. A 2019 review found "some support for seasonal variation in clinical depression" but noted that prior research was "fragmented," with varied findings.

Multiple studies have documented that heat can affect mood disorders and behavior, says Kim Meidenbauer, an assistant professor of psychology at Washington State University, who studies heat's psychological effects. Increases in aggression and violent crimes have been well documented on hotter days and during summertime, Meidenbauer says. Recent studies have also found that psychiatric emergency room visits for depression and other mental health disorders peak on hotter days, mood trends more negative with increased heat and suicide rates rise in conjunction with temperature. The latter study on suicide risk, which was published in 2018, also found a decline in well-being corresponding to hotter outdoor temperatures, according to an accompanying analysis of depressive language in 600 million posts on Twitter (now X) between May 2014 and July 2015.

Rosenthal notes the findings about psychiatric hospital admissions, suicide risk and even online activity are in line with his previous work on SAD, which also concluded that people who face mental health struggles in the summer are more agitated than those who do so in the winter. People who are depressed but restless—with energy to spare—might be more likely to act on suicidal urges or end up in the hospital or, he explains.

Meidenbauer notes there are a few hypotheses for why heat might trigger depression. For one, "it interrupts your sleep," she says—and quality shut-eye is critical for mental health. Maintaining a normal body temperature is also a resource-intensive process, Meidenbauer says. Heat can become a physical stressor, particularly for children, older people and those taking certain medications that disrupt the body's ability to cool down. If people are uncomfortable over a long period of time, that invariably affects emotional state, she says.

One 2018 review study indicates that heat may also disrupt neurotransmitters involved in brain activity while we're awake, which could contribute to depression. In addition, multiple studies have found that depressed people have an elevated body temperature, especially at night, which suggests depression itself may undermine the body's ability to regulate temperature.

Wehr says investigating the relationship between temperature and mental health could help home in on the mechanisms underlying depression and even improve treatments, which is especially important because experts overwhelmingly agree that climate change is likely to exacerbate the mental health risks of hot weather.

Summer SAD Solutions

Treatments for summer depression are understudied, Rohan says. There is some evidence that lowering the body temperature via air-conditioning, cold showers or swimming sessions can help at least temporarily. In Rosenthal and Wehr's first case report, one patient's mood improved when Wehr recommended she try confining herself to an air-conditioned house and regularly taking cold showers, but she reported feeling depressed again just nine days after stopping this regimen.

Meidenbauer points out that staying indoors in heavily air-conditioned spaces and taking frequent cold showers likely isn't sustainable from an environmental, practical or financial perspective. Swamp coolers and fans may be cheaper, more accessible options—particularly for that extra critical nighttime cooling.

Counterintuitively, exposure to high heat via saunas and hot tubs might offer longer-term relief. Some clinical trials have found that peoples' depression improved when treated with hot baths. This could be because short-duration, high-intensity heat resets dormant or dysfunctional thermoregulatory systems in people with depression, says Ashley Mason, a clinical psychologist and an associate professor at the University of California, San Francisco. If people with summer SAD have thermoregulation issues, Mason suggests, such heat therapies may be especially helpful.

Beyond manipulating body temperature, simply tracking mood and comfort level throughout the summer season can be useful, Meidenbauer says. Noticing a pattern is the first step toward changing it, she adds. If you know that heat dampens your mood, that's one more tool you can use to potentially predict, prepare for and mitigate (metaphorically) dark days. Rosenthal agrees. "Look at the things that make you feel better and do them more. And look at the things that make you feel worse and do them less," he says. This tip can help people who experience mental health issues any time of year.

If you or someone you know is struggling or having thoughts of suicide, help is available. Call or text the 988 Suicide & Crisis Lifeline at 988 or use the online Lifeline Chat.

About the Author

Lauren Leffer is a contributing writer and former tech reporting fellow at Scientific American. *She covers many subjects, including artificial intelligence, climate and weird biology, because she's curious to a fault. Follow her on X @lauren_leffer and on Bluesky @laurenleffer.bsky.social.*

Why Just One Sleepless Night Makes People Emotionally Fragile

By Eti Ben Simon

When I was a graduate student, my colleagues and I studied how losing one night of sleep affects a person's ability to manage their emotions. Once a week, typically on a Friday evening, I would stay up all night to monitor our participants and ensure that they followed the protocol. At about noon the next day, we would all stumble out of the laboratory, exhausted and eager to get home and rest.

Two months into the experiment, I was in my car at a traffic light when a silly love song started playing on the radio. Suddenly, I was crying uncontrollably. I remember feeling surprised at my reaction. It then hit me that I was not just studying sleep deprivation—I had become *part* of the study. Weeks of missed sleep had taken their toll, and I was no longer in control of my emotions.

That research project, and many that have followed since, demonstrated a strong and intimate link between better sleep and emotional health. In healthy individuals, good-quality sleep is linked with a more positive mood—and it takes just one night of sleep deprivation to trigger a robust spike in anxiety and depression the following morning. Moreover, people who suffer from chronic sleep disruption tend to experience daily events as more negative, making it hard to escape a gloomy mindset. Indeed, in a national sleep survey, 85 percent of Americans reported mood disruption when they were not able to get enough sleep.

Studies from our lab and others are now beginning to illuminate just how a lack of sleep frays the inner fabric of our mind. One of its many impacts is to disrupt the brain's circuitry for regulating emotions.

For decades researchers and medical professionals considered sleep loss a by-product or symptom of another, more "primary" condition, such as depression or anxiety. In other words, *first* comes the anxiety, and then sleep loss follows. Today we know that this order can be reversed. In fact, sleep loss and anxiety, depression or other mental health conditions may feed into one another, creating a downward spiral that is exceedingly difficult to break.

Much evidence in this area comes from chronic sleeplessness or insomnia. People who suffer from insomnia are at least twice as likely to develop depression or anxiety later in life, compared with individuals who sleep well. For instance, a study that followed 1,500 individuals—some with insomnia and others without—found that chronic sleeplessness was associated with a three times greater increase in the onset of depression a year later and twice the increase in the onset of anxiety.

Insomnia symptoms also raise the risk of developing post-traumatic stress disorder and track closely with suicidal behavior among at-risk individuals. They often precede a mood episode in people with bipolar disorder. Even after adequate treatment for depression or anxiety, people who continue to suffer from sleep difficulties are at greater risk of relapse relative to those whose sleep improves. Understanding sleep's role in this pattern could unlock insights for helping to prevent and treat many emotional and mental disorders.

Older research already revealed that sleep loss can precede serious mental health symptoms in otherwise healthy individuals. In studies conducted mostly in the 1960s, volunteers who stayed awake for more than two nights reported difficulties forming thoughts, finding words and composing sentences. They suffered from hallucinations, such as seeing inanimate objects move or experiencing the sensation of another's touch despite being alone. After three days without sleep, some participants became delusional and paranoid. They believed they were secret agents or that aliens were contacting them. (If that sounds like a psychotic episode, that's because it is.) After five days, several participants entered a state resembling a full-blown clinical psychosis and were unable to fully comprehend their circumstances.

In one study from 1947, volunteers from the U.S. military attempted to stay awake for more than four nights. A soldier who was described by his friends as quiet and reserved became extremely aggressive after three nights without sleep. He provoked fights and insisted he was on a secret mission for the president. Eventually he was forcibly restrained and dismissed from the experiment. Six others exhibited outbursts of violence and persistent hallucinations. In all cases, after sleeping for an entire day, the soldiers behaved normally again and had no recollection of the earlier mayhem. In another study, in which participants stayed awake for four nights, researchers were unprepared for the "frequent psychotic features" they encountered, such as intense hallucinations and paranoid delusions.

Given these destructive effects, studies of prolonged sleep loss are now considered to be unethical, but they still offer a powerful reminder of just how sleep-dependent our minds and mental health truly are.

Even with these startling results, scientists have been skeptical about the consequences of restless nights, particularly given that (fortunately) few of us endure such extreme deprivation. That's where the newest wave of research comes in. In recent years a neuroscientific explanation has emerged that is beginning to illuminate what it is about sleep, or the lack of it, that seems to have a direct link to our emotions.

Whenever we face a nerve-wracking or emotionally intense challenge, a hub deep in the brain called the amygdala kicks into gear. The amygdala can trigger a comprehensive whole-body response to prepare us for the challenge or threat we face. This flight-or-fight response increases our heart rate and sends a wave of stress hormones rushing into our bloodstream. Luckily, there's one brain region standing between us and this cascade of hyperarousal: the prefrontal cortex, an area right behind the middle of our eyebrows. Studies show that activity in this region tends to dampen, or downregulate, the amygdala, thus keeping our emotional response under control.

In studies where my colleagues and I deprived healthy volunteers of one night of sleep, they discovered that the activity of the prefrontal cortex dropped drastically, as measured using functional magnetic resonance imaging (fMRI). Moreover, the neural activity linking the amygdala and the prefrontal cortex became significantly weaker. In other words, both the region and the circuit meant to keep our emotional reactions under control are essentially out of order when sleep is disrupted. Other studies have found that this profile of neural impairment can occur in people after they experience just one night of sleep deprivation, in people who are habitual short sleepers, or when participants' sleep is restricted to only four hours a night for five nights.

This impairment can be so robust that it blurs the lines around what people consider emotional. For example, when my colleagues and I exposed participants to neutral and emotional pictures (think bland images of commuters on a train versus photographs of children crying), fMRI revealed that the amygdala responded differently to these prompts when people were well rested. But after losing a night of sleep, a person's amygdala responded strongly to *both* kinds of images. In other words, the threshold for what the brain deems emotional became significantly lower when the amygdala could not act in concert with the prefrontal cortex. Such impaired emotional control makes us more vulnerable to anxiety and poor mood, so that even silly love songs can trigger sobbing.

The effects on the amygdala, the prefrontal cortex and the circuitry between the two may have many other consequences as well. In January we published findings that show that changes in this brain circuit, together with other regions involved in arousal, relate to increases in blood pressure after one night of sleep loss. The brain-level mechanisms my colleagues and I have observed may contribute to changes that negatively affect the entire body, increasing the risk for hypertension and cardiovascular disease.

Stepping back, it becomes clear that—like our physical well-being—mental and emotional health rely on a delicate balance. Myriad choices we make throughout the day *and* night maintain that balance. Even a single sleepless night can therefore do damage. We need to be mindful of this reality, for both ourselves and one another. Inevitably we all miss out on sleep from time to time. But our societies should critically examine structures—such as work norms, school cultures, and the lack of support for parents or other caregivers—that prevent people from getting enough rest. The science of sleep and mental health suggests that failing to address those problems will leave people vulnerable to serious harm.

About the Author

Eti Ben Simon is a research scientist at the University of California, Berkeley. She studies the emotional and social consequences of sleep loss on the human brain and body.

Losing a Grandparent Hurts Boys at School

By Michelle S. Livings, Emily Smith-Greenaway, Rachel Margolis & Ashton M. Verdery

Death is not random. Demographers estimate that 75 percent of Americans are expected to live to age 70, meaning that most deaths occur late in life. The death of an older relative, such as a grandparent, is expected. As such, a grandparent's death is considered part of life and not an event with consequences that ripple through space and time. But what if this is a misconception?

Historically, there has not been much research on this topic. Social scientists have tended to downplay grandparental death as a potentially significant event in a young person's life. Scholars have long taken interest in adverse consequences of deaths viewed as more traumatic, such as those of a parent, sibling or child. But grandparental deaths are almost never studied—despite being at least 10 times more common than any other losses for people under age 20. Perhaps this reflects the general view that grandparent deaths are just part of life, an excuse to miss gym class or an inconvenient exam.

A closer look at the death of grandparents, however, reveals that the impact of their loss is very real and can be harmful for boys in particular. Our research shows that losing a grandparent hurts boys in school at a critical time in their life, and this is especially the case for Black and Hispanic boys.

Approximately 7.3 million children—about 10 percent of U.S. kids—live with their grandparents, a phenomenon that is especially common among Asian, Hispanic, Black and other minority populations, as well as among families with less education and fewer resources. But it is far from rare in any demographic groups. Social scientists overlooking grandparental death contrasts with robust findings emphasizing the importance of grandparents in the lives of their grandchildren, especially when grandkids live with single moms. Grandparents often help with childcare, financial support and housing, all essential to their grandchildren's development and well-being. A grandparent's death can ripple throughout a family, influencing not only a grandchild directly but also their parents' mental health, behavior and even economic and relationship stability.

Given how common grandparental death is, and with good reason to expect that such a loss might carry hidden costs, we set out to understand whether and how young grandchildren respond. Our suspicion, based on the vital roles grandparents play in their grandchildren's lives, was that their death would disrupt their grandchildren's healthy development. We wanted to go beyond looking at feelings of sadness, or even the somewhat rarer development of psychological disorders. Therefore, we focused on more intermediate outcomes, including cognitive development, school performance and ultimately the mastering of academic skills.

We used a national dataset of pairs of mothers and children interviewed multiple times since the child's birth. This dataset focuses on diverse family circumstances, including large proportions of children of color born to unmarried, less-educated mothers, allowing us to examine kids who we expected might be most affected by losing a grandparent. We used standard assessment tools to measure whether the death of a grandparent in early or middle childhood affected a nine-year-old grandchild's academic performance, including math skills, reading comprehension and verbal skills, reflecting their command of grammar and vocabulary.

Overwhelmingly, our study shows that the loss of a grandparent harms the academic performance of boys. Boys who recently lost their grandmother had lower verbal skills, compared with their peers whose grandmothers were still alive, and boys whose grandfathers died earlier in childhood had lower math skills, reading comprehension and verbal skills, compared with their peers whose grandfathers were still alive. In contrast, we found no differences in girls' academic skills following the death of a maternal grandparent, compared with girls whose grandparents were still alive. Although our data do not allow us to confirm what is driving these gender differences, we suspect that gender socialization, which can result in boys feeling that grieving and being sad are not "masculine" behaviors (and thus are not appropriate for boys), can harm these boys' school performance.

Because of racial differences in children's school and family environments, we took this analysis a step further and examined whether Black, Hispanic and white children had distinct experiences after losing a grandparent (too few Asian children were in the dataset for us to explore). Overall, the findings suggest that boys of color suffer the worst impacts. Black boys had lower verbal skills after the recent death of a grandparent, and Hispanic boys had lower math skills, reading comprehension and verbal skills after losing their grandfather in either early or middle childhood.

Our results provide cause for concern. As of November 2023, an estimated 4.6 million Americans have lost a grandparent as a consequence of COVID. When we think about the impact of COVID on school-age kids, we tend to focus on school closures and their consequences for youth learning and socialization. But considering the large number of excess deaths related to COVID—and the large number of grandchildren who have lost a grandparent to COVID—our study suggests that a "double dose" of learning loss and stalled academic development is underway for many children. Beyond COVID, our study suggests a massive population of children might be harmed by an event many think of as harmless. After all, our estimates suggest that anywhere from 10 million to 12.5 million Americans lose a grandparent each year even without this novel disease.

For most of the year, schools are essential safety nets for supporting kids. Although grief interventions have been tested in some, broad implementation of such programs is necessary. School counselors can also help bereaved children grieve while continuing to excel academically. Even so, policy makers, health professionals and educators need to think more broadly about this phenomenon. This is of critical importance for future generations, given that mastery of these fundamental academic skills early in life is predictive of numerous outcomes in adulthood.

Losing a grandparent may be a rite of passage, but it is not harmless. Our study suggests the death of a grandparent is harmful for many boys, and this is particularly true for boys of color. Society has traditionally focused on some losses as more worthy of sympathy and consideration—but our research emphasizes the need to recognize that any exposure to death, especially in childhood, is a possible source of adversity.

This is an opinion and analysis article, and the views expressed by the author or authors are not necessarily those of Scientific American.

About the Authors

Michelle S. Livings is a postdoctoral research associate the Center for Research on Child and Family Wellbeing at Princeton University.

Emily Smith-Greenaway is a professor of sociology and spatial sciences at the Dornsife College of Letters, Arts and Sciences at the University of Southern California.

Rachel Margolis is a professor of sociology at the University of Western Ontario.

Ashton M. Verdery is an associate professor of sociology, demography and social data analytics and a co-hire faculty of the Institute for Computational and Data Sciences at Pennsylvania State University.

Aggression Disorders Are Serious, Stigmatized, and Treatable

By Abigail Marsh

R oughly every month I receive an e-mail from a parent somewhere in the world asking for help with a child who is violent, angry or aggressive. Some people describe being physically beaten or having their life threatened by their son or daughter. These families may spend thousands of dollars on special schools and treatments. Often they are desperate, afraid and looking for guidance.

Psychologists recognize several conditions that are characterized by violence and aggression. They include conduct disorder and disruptive mood dysregulation disorder in children as well as antisocial personality disorder in adults. To this list I would add psychopathy, which is assessed using different criteria than those used to diagnose antisocial personality disorder—though it is not an official diagnosis in the fifth edition of the *Diagnostic and Statistical Manual of Mental Disorders*.

Although each of these conditions differs from the others in important ways, all are defined by the fact that affected individuals engage in persistent, severe antisocial or aggressive behaviors. Children diagnosed with conduct disorder or disruptive mood dysregulation disorder, for example, may be physically violent or display bursts of destructive anger. These disorders, which are characterized by patterns of exploitative, hurtful or cruel behavior, place children at risk for developing antisocial personality disorder or psychopathy when they grow up.

These disorders are not rare. Conduct disorder affects up to 9 percent of girls and up to 16 percent of boys. Its symptoms, such as stealing and deliberately harming people or animals, are among the most common reasons for referring children for mental health treatment. And antisocial personality disorder is estimated to affect one in 50 people, making it more prevalent than schizophrenia, bipolar disorder or anorexia.

Given the prevalence and severity of these conditions, you might think abundant resources exist to help affected adults and children, but that is not the case. Relative to other common, serious mental disorders, disorders of aggression are underdiagnosed, undertreated and underrecognized. And that is not because these disorders cannot be accurately diagnosed and successfully treated—they can. New research is providing clinicians and scientists more insight than ever before into how these conditions develop and how to intervene. And the earlier in life treatment begins, the more successful it tends to be.

But these disorders are terribly stigmatized, leading well-meaning clinicians to avoid diagnosing them and many patients and parents to refuse to accept them. The fact that generations of psychologists have invoked unhelpful moralistic frameworks—essentially condemning people with these disorders as "bad" or even "evil"—has only added to the intense negative judgment of these conditions. Even some mental health organizations, both private and public, avoid mentioning them.

We now know, however, that these disorders are true illnesses that reflect dysfunctional patterns of brain structure and function that lead to maladaptive thoughts and emotions and ultimately aggressive or violent behavior. These problems result from the combined influence of genetic risk factors and environmental stressors. Contrary to previous assumptions, they are not simply the result of "bad parenting"—an idea that has brought harm and shame to families. Varied factors, including birth complications, trauma and exposure to toxins such as lead, may contribute—though for many people, no clear stressor is ever identified. In addition, without treatment, these disorders will likely persist or worsen.

Symptoms often emerge early in life and continue over time. A study conducted by researchers in Cyprus, Belgium and Sweden and published last May tracked more than 2,000 children over the course of 10 years, collecting parent and teacher reports at five different time points between the ages of three and 13. The analysis revealed that an early emerging risk factor for later antisocial behavior was a fearless temperament, which often manifests as insensitivity to risk or harm in preschool-aged children. That trait can make children very difficult to parent because they do not learn to avoid risky, dangerous behaviors or behaviors that could result in punishment.

Perhaps unsurprisingly, the study also found that children with this temperament tended to experience harsher parenting and more conflict with their parents over time. They also developed "callous-unemotional traits," such as low empathy and remorse, which can further increase the risk for antisocial behaviors. Fearless temperaments may lead to low empathy in part because children who themselves do not feel fear strongly struggle to empathize with this emotion in others. Over time, "maladaptive fearlessness" can increase the risk of antisocial and criminal behavior in adulthood.

Given these tendencies, punishment does not improve behavior in children and adults with these illnesses. In fact, disorders characterized by aggression are often linked to *less responsiveness* to punishment, no matter how harsh, making it a futile response to aggression. Last July researchers in Germany, the U.K. and the Netherlands published findings from an experiment that examined how 92 children and adolescents with conduct disorder learned from punishment, compared with 130 of their typically developing peers. The children played a simple game in which they had to learn to select images that would result in a reward (gain of points) versus punishment (loss of points). As the game progressed, most children learned to avoid the images that result in punishment. But those with conduct disorder persisted in choosing these images more often, despite showing normal rates of learning from reward. This suggests that fundamental neurodevelopmental deficits in learning about punishment and risk underlie the emergence of serious antisocial behavior.

Though harsh punishment is ineffective for treating disorders of aggression, there are interventions that do help. In March 2023 another group published an analysis that pooled data from 60 studies that assessed the success of treatment for children with serious disruptive behavior disorders such as conduct disorder. The findings revealed that a range of treatment types were effective in improving children's symptoms—contrary to the prevalent myth that these disorders are untreatable.

The most effective approaches for severely affected children (those with callous-unemotional traits) were focused on training parents. In such treatments, which include parent management training and parent-child interaction therapy, therapists teach parents to use specific therapeutic techniques to reduce children's symptoms and improve their social skills and relationships. Consistent with the research on rewards and punishment, the therapeutic approaches that emphasize rewarding desired behaviors—and withholding rewards when children act out—are most effective. In general, these types of treatments should be considered first-line therapy for children with antisocial behavior, although too often they are not offered to families who could benefit from them.

Even the most seriously affected adults can improve with evidence-based treatment. A study published last year examined the effects of a treatment called schema therapy on more than 100 people convicted of violent offences in Dutch high-security forensic hospitals. All of these people had diagnoses of personality disorders such as antisocial personality disorder or narcissistic personality disorder. Schema therapy involves identifying and replacing maladaptive patterns of thinking, feeling and relating to others. Patients treated with this therapy showed more improvement in their symptoms and moved more rapidly through rehabilitation than those who received standard individual or group therapy. This work suggests that rehabilitation is possible and could yield enormous potential savings in costs related to incarceration, as well as significant gains in public health and safety.

Of course, all of these treatments hinge on accurate diagnosis. My colleagues and I have found that children diagnosed with conduct disorder and callous-unemotional traits (which are also called "limited prosocial emotions") show *opposite* patterns of brain dysfunction compared with children who have conduct disorder as a result of anxiety or trauma. This finding indicates that these groups of kids would likely benefit from completely different treatments, despite some overlap in their symptoms, which brings us back again to the urgent need to improve the recognition, discussion and accurate diagnosis of these disorders.

Many different steps are needed. For one, all major mental health organizations must give recognized disorders of aggression explicit parity with other mental disorders. Even today, someone who seeks information about conduct disorder, psychopathy or antisocial personality disorder may search the websites of major organizations such as the National Institute of Mental Health or the National Alliance on Mental Illness in vain. This information gap was a major reason my colleagues and I came together to found Psychopathy Is, an organization dedicated to providing information and resources about psychopathy, a major contributor to many forms of antisociality in both children and adults, including bullying, domestic assault and gun violence.

In addition, much more can be done to improve professional training and guidelines. And public and private mental health organizations must devote as many resources to screening tools, interventions and studies of the causes of disorders of aggression as they do to similarly common and serious disorders, such as autism and attention deficit hyperactivity disorder. With more research will come better understanding, better treatments and hope for a full and productive life for affected children and adults. Though these changes wouldn't yield instantaneous gains, they would represent a more compassionate and—most importantly—more effective approach to helping people, including the many families in need of answers.

This is an opinion and analysis article, and the views expressed by the author or authors are not necessarily those of Scientific American.

About the Author

Abigail Marsh is a psychologist and neuroscientist at Georgetown University, where she directs the Laboratory on Social & Affective Neuroscience.

Section 3: Environmental Impact

Air Pollution Is Really Dangerous, Even More Evidence Shows

By Jesse Greenspan

A ir pollution is one of the world's greatest public health threats, reducing global life expectancy more than smoking, alcohol or childhood malnutrition. Recent studies estimate that fine particulate matter called $PM_{2.5}$–pumped out by cars, factories, woodstoves and wildfires–causes nearly nine million premature deaths annually, with South Asia bearing the highest tolls.

$PM_{2.5}$ particles are tiny enough to enter the bloodstream and lodge in the lungs, where they contribute to respiratory problems such as asthma. They also can prompt heart attacks and strokes. And they have been linked to diabetes, obesity and dementia and may exacerbate COVID. As several recent studies demonstrate, the consequences of dirty air don't stop there. "We are finding out that particulate matter affects almost every aspect of our bodies and minds, from cognition to our heartbeats to our skin," says Christa Hasenkopf, an air-quality data expert at the University of Chicago. Though not involved in the three studies highlighted here, Hasenkopf expresses no surprise at the results, which "underscore literally thousands of other studies that show similar conclusions."

Cancer

Living near high-traffic roadways or other areas rife with $PM_{2.5}$ increases the risk of breast cancer by about 8 percent, according to a study that examined 15,870 breast cancer patients in six U.S. states and two cities. Lead author Alexandra White, an epidemiologist at the National Institute of Environmental Health Sciences, speculates that airborne pollutants make people more susceptible to breast cancer by disrupting "the normal hormonal mechanisms in our bodies." White is also studying air pollution's impact on gynecological cancers, and other researchers have tied it to liver, pancreatic, prostate, lung and ovarian cancers, among others.

Smaller Babies

Along with the elderly and already ill, babies tend to suffer the most from air pollution; it has been shown to impair their lungs, their immune responses and even their size. Women in northern Europe exposed to $PM_{2.5}$ and other air pollutants give birth to smaller babies, according to findings that Robin Mzati Sinsamala, an epidemiologist at Norway's University of Bergen, presented recently at a European Respiratory Society conference. Fine particles can penetrate the placenta and affect the "exchange of oxygen and nutrients between the baby and the mother," Sinsamala says, noting that infants with low birth weights face many health risks.

Suicide

In the U.S., smoke from increasingly large and frequent wildfires impacts more than just physical health. David Molitor, an associate professor of finance at the University of Illinois at Urbana-Champaign, and his colleagues have found that the number of suicides ticks up in rural U.S. counties (though not urban ones) on smoky days. "It adds a little extra stress," Molitor says, "and sometimes that's all that's needed if you're in a vulnerable position to begin with."

If you or someone you know is struggling or having thoughts of suicide, help is available. Call or text the 988 Suicide & Crisis Lifeline at 988 or use the online Lifeline Chat.

About the Author

Jesse Greenspan is a San Francisco Bay Area–based freelance journalist who writes about history and the environment.

Treating Mental Health as Part of Climate Disaster Recovery

By Anna Mattson

The U.S. has had an unprecedented year of climate disasters—a relentless whirlwind of droughts, floods, cyclones and wildfires costing billions of dollars. Catastrophic events such as the firestorm in Hawaii and Hurricane Idalia in Florida have been battering down the homes and livelihoods of countless people, leaving trails of long-lasting destruction across the country.

Marty Dwyer, a disaster mental health supervisor with the American Red Cross, says the psychological impact of such sudden and massive losses can make it especially difficult to make big decisions in the aftermath, when they are often most urgently needed. And a hugely consequential choice immediately faces most survivors when they return to their destroyed homes: Should they stay and rebuild or migrate to someplace that seems safer?

"Whether you are a person experiencing homelessness or transiently unhoused because of disaster, that is a risk [to mental health]," says Joshua Morganstein, chair of the American Psychiatric Association's Committee on the Psychiatric Dimensions of Disaster. Morganstein has worked with survivors of mass shootings, Hurricane Katrina and various wildfires and has witnessed firsthand how disaster trauma impacts mental wellbeing.

A growing body of research is revealing how crises of climate change—including wildfire smoke, pollution, flooding and extreme heat—are worsening conditions such as anxiety, depression and post-traumatic stress disorder (PTSD). While experts emphasize the importance of quickly getting people rehoused, rebuilding in a disaster-prone area could subject people to the trauma of losing their home yet again.

Scientific American spoke with Morganstein and Dwyer about the correlation between housing and mental health post-disaster and about measures to prevent repeated traumatization as these disasters persist.

[An edited transcript of the interview follows.]

SA: How does climate disaster trauma differ from other kinds and symptoms of trauma?

Dwyer: A climate disaster raises the level of trauma significantly when people don't have a chance to prepare and wait. For example, with the wildfire in Maui, they basically had no notice. But in all disasters, you see some pretty similar responses: people might be feeling just absolutely overwhelmed or numb or experiencing high levels of anxiety. It's not uncommon for people to be very angry.

The first things I see are more physical complaints. People describe having insomnia, diminished appetite, headaches or stomachaches. On top of that, many people have preexisting mental health conditions or they have had prior trauma that makes them more likely to need additional assistance.

Morganstein: People who are exposed to any given disaster have different types of exposure. Many people experience distress, annoyances and general stressors. And there can be many of those that pile up on top of one another. Of course, the stresses that people experience change over time. The stresses of the moment of a hurricane are very different from the stress of two weeks, six weeks, six months and 12 months after the event.

Immediate stress reactions include feeling unsafe, which causes significant negative health effects. People who feel unsafe, for instance, are more likely to have difficulty with sleep, and they're more likely to increase their use of alcohol and tobacco. They're also more likely to indicate symptoms of general distress.

Some people may ultimately develop psychiatric disorders. Most often we think about PTSD in the event of a disaster. PTSD is not the most frequent disorder, however. Depression is more common.

It's hard enough to move to a new place when you *want* to, and you've planned for it, and all of your possessions are with you. But people who have been forcefully displaced are dealing with issues of grief, which is a very overlooked but universal response to disasters. It's often the thing that hangs on for people long after scars are healed. Mental health professionals will diagnose depression, anxiety or PTSD. But we as a society do not do a very good job, I think, at anticipating and addressing the almost universal issue of grief that happens in the wake of all disaster events.

SA: Why is housing important to mental health in post-disaster relief?

Morganstein: There are negative physical health and mental health effects that become enhanced when people are unhoused.

Many people who are displaced find themselves in shelters, makeshift or otherwise, with a bunch of strangers. They are without comfort or things that make them feel safe—such as a locked door or just some place to go where they don't feel exposed to other people. People have difficulty sleeping in loud, noisy places, and they're limited in their ability to protect whatever property they're able to take. When someone has chronically underslept, almost everything in their life gets worse: their ability to make decisions, to exercise good judgment, to take protective actions, to assess threats properly in ways that protect themselves and their family.

In an attempt to address that, hotels have offered support and have tried to be good stewards in their community after disasters. They move people into their facilities. Being in a place where your family can go and be together and lock a door will help some people to feel safer. People find they can connect with, learn from or share adversity with others who are going through this difficult situation. But one of the things that this might also do is lead some people to feel isolated. Different people have different needs.

Dwyer: Housing is very, very important. One of the things we have seen, especially during the COVID pandemic, is that organizations in the U.S. seem to be getting people out of congregate group shelters and moving towards what we refer to as "noncongregate shelters" [such as hotels]. It might not be home, but it's not a large building where you're sleeping right next to strangers.

SA: What are some pros and cons of staying and rebuilding?

Morganstein: Some people leave because they feel a sense of threat and feel unsafe. Disasters often do not just take people out of their home but also scatter the community. Everyone disperses because their communities were wiped out by a tornado, hurricane or wildfire. Everyone had to move. Now all of that support is sort of gone. It's probably important to think about the extent to which people choose to stay versus people who simply do not have the means or resources to go [who say] "I'm here because I have no other choice."

For others, staying can be a way to build a sense of resilience. It can be a path to recovery to go back to and to be present in a place where something difficult happened. We have to remember that most people, even people who have difficulties along the way, will ultimately be okay—and this is very important. Eventually people are able to make meaning of those events. And at some point, people can look hopefully to the future.

SA: How can people rebuilding in disaster-sensitive areas prevent retraumatization?

Morganstein: The fundamental framework for interventions that we know protect mental health, foster resilience and improve people's ability to function after disasters involves five essential elements: enhancing a sense of safety, calming, social connectedness, self- or community efficacy and hope. Before it gets to the point where we're talking about medications and therapies, fostering those five essential elements really is the framework for protecting people who are experiencing extreme stress.

We also want to remind people of their innate strengths and capabilities. When we see someone doing something, our goal is not to take over and do everything for a person. We might feel, "Oh, my gosh, this person has been through so much. I'm just going to help them." Unfortunately, when we do everything for someone, the feeling of helplessness can almost be exacerbated. Helping someone to know where to go encourages them to take those steps. Lower those barriers for people who are having a lot of difficulties.

Is it going to be worse or better? I'd like to be able to give you a simple answer to whether people should come back. The reality is that there are many factors for individuals that will likely come into play. I do think it's important to think about—because these events are happening more frequently.

If you simply search the literature for "repeat disasters," there isn't a lot out there to show what happens over time for people who are exposed to events over and over again. Certainly we have some evidence to show that after difficult situations, people learn from them and feel better equipped to handle them in the future.

Dwyer: Our goal is not to replace the community resources. We are there to supplement and strengthen what the local community has in place, especially in places such as Hawaii or Puerto Rico, where the culture is so important. We want people to get support in a culturally sensitive way. We come from all over; we don't necessarily know what it's like to live in that community.

If you can alleviate immediate emotional distress, it really does make a difference. Most individuals and families are able to function adequately after a disaster. They may not be as effective in their daily activities. They may have difficulty processing and problem solving, for example. But most people, as devastating as [the disaster] seems, are able to move forward. We help them to discover their resilience and take those first steps.

About the Author

Anna Mattson is a freelance science journalist based in South Dakota. You can find more of her work at annamattson.com or follow her on Twitter @AnnaMattson9.

Americans Have Breathed More Wildfire Smoke in Eight Months Than in Entire Years

By Meghan Bartles

The average American may have already inhaled more wildfire smoke in the first eight months of this year than during any recent full year.

What's responsible for the record? Canada's unprecedented blazes, which began in late April, have sent plumes of smoke south to the U.S., impacting communities in the Midwest and along the East Coast that are unaccustomed to wildfires. This event is undermining a decades-long trend toward generally cleaner air in the U.S., driven by decades of reduced anthropogenic pollution. Now experts hope the shock of 2023's smoke will inspire collective and individual actions to reduce future wildfire smoke exposure.

This year "fire activity has been near historic lows in most of the western U.S.," says Marshall Burke, an economist at Stanford University. "Yet this will likely be the worst wildfire smoke year on record in the U.S. and [is] entirely due to Canadian fires. So that's really new."

Burke and his colleagues calculated that by early July, the average American had been exposed to nearly 450 micrograms of smoke per cubic meter ($\mu g/m3$). When they ran the same analysis back to 2006, they found the largest exposure of those years came in 2021. Over the course of that year, the average American was exposed to just more than 400 $\mu g/m3$, in part because of a particularly active fire season in the Rocky Mountains. The years 2020 and 2022 also brought significantly above-average smoke exposure, which was driven by fires in the western U.S. as well.

"That increase in wildfire exposure is really reflective of not just more fires but more fires lasting for longer and impacting large population areas—so just more people being exposed to more smoke for longer periods of time," says Delphine Farmer, an atmospheric chemist at Colorado State University, who was not involved in the exposure analysis. "That trend has been increasing over the last decade, and I am unsurprised that we are hitting a maximum this year."

Burke and his colleagues relied on satellite data first gathered in 2006 to figure out where smoky skies predominated. By combining those data with general air pollution measurements from sensors on the ground, they could calculate how much of the smoke was low in the atmosphere, where people can breathe it in. Finally, the researchers incorporated local population density to determine about how much smoke Americans were breathing.

The approach isn't perfect, Burke and others note—surface sensors don't distinguish between wildfire smoke and other types of small particle pollution, such as that from local factories. And some experts question whether, for example, a median analysis that would be less influenced by outliers would be a more meaningful approach than the national average.

But the calculation is one way to illustrate the extraordinary nature of this year's fire season, Burke says.

Typically U.S. wildfires—and the smoke they create—are contained in the West. But this year a wet winter has led to below-average fire activity in the West, while Canada has seen more than 5,000 fires burn more than 13 million hectares, according to Natural Resources Canada. Weather patterns have sporadically funneled smoke from fires in eastern Canada south over the densely populated Eastern Seaboard, quickly exposing large numbers of people to high levels of smoke, albeit briefly.

"What's troubling about this event is that so many, many people were affected," says Loretta Mickley, an atmospheric chemist at Harvard University, who wasn't involved in the exposure estimate.

With more than 120 million people in the eastern and Midwestern U.S. exposed to that smoke, this year's average exposure soared, Burke says.

Wildfire smoke contains tiny particles that can travel deep into the body and wreak havoc, particularly on the respiratory and cardiac systems, says Carrie Redlich, a pulmonologist and occupational environmental medicine physician at the Yale School of Medicine, who wasn't involved in the exposure analysis. There's still a lot that doctors don't know about the impacts of wildfire smoke, however. Much of the research is based on general air pollution, and it's difficult to tease apart the role smoke played in any given health outcome, Redlich says.

The impacts of short bursts of high smoke exposure are even trickier to pinpoint. "For any given person, it's not like their two days [of wildfire smoke are] going to give them lung cancer versus not," Redlich says. "But when you multiply the risk over millions of people, which is what's happened, then there is the public health [concern]."

Christa Hasenkopf, an air quality data expert at the University of Chicago, who calculates the impact of air pollution on life expectancy, says that it takes about two weeks of high air pollution to start to see health impacts in these analyses. But she also emphasizes that some of the worst air quality in the U.S. this summer is a regular occurrence in places such as Delhi. Globally, she says, air pollution reduced life expectancy in 2020 by an average of about 2.2 years. In the U.S. that number was 2.5 months, and the county with the worst air that year—Mariposa County, California—would experience a 1.7-year decrease in life expectancy if those conditions became the norm.

Experts also underscore that even during a remarkably bad year for wildfire smoke, U.S. air is much cleaner than it has been. "Most of the measures would suggest that, on average, the air is still much cleaner than it was even 15 years ago or definitely 30 years ago," Burke says.

"The background story here, which is really important, is the monumental success we have had in improving air quality," he says. But if smoke worsens, he warns, that overall picture might start to shift. "Wildfires are really pushing back on that pretty hard."

Burke says that the same Clean Air Act legislation that cleaned up power production and vehicles could be adapted to tackle wildfire smoke, including by encouraging prescribed burns. These purposefully set and carefully monitored fires can reduce the odds of large, uncontrollable blazes by burning through fuel.

Farmer says she hopes this year's high smoke exposure will encourage just such activities. "We also need to realize that we have the opportunity to change and impact our wildfire smoke exposure, and we have tools that we can use," Farmer says. Even individuals can take action to reduce their exposure by using purifiers—even homemade ones—to clean indoor air.

"Could there be a dystopian future? Well, yes, there could," Farmer says. "But I think we have to look at it from the perspective that we have tools we can implement to avoid that. I really hope that this summer is a wake-up call to policymakers and politicians and the public in general to start thinking about those tools."

About the Author

Meghan Bartels is a science journalist based in New York City. She joined Scientific American in 2023 and is now a senior news reporter there. Previously, she spent more than four years as a writer and editor at Space.com, as well as nearly a year as a science reporter at Newsweek, where she focused on space and Earth science. Her writing has also appeared in Audubon, Nautilus, Astronomy and Smithsonian, among other publications. She attended Georgetown University and earned a master's degree in journalism at New York University's Science, Health and Environmental Reporting Program.

Wildfires and Smoke Are Harming People's Mental Health. Here's How to Cope

By Stephanie Pappas

If you have been in the path of the smoke from wildfires in Canada this month—or if you've been caught up in wildfire smoke before—you may have experienced feelings of anxiety and claustrophobia as the skies turned an apocalyptic orange.

It's a common reaction and an understandable one, says Thomas Joseph Doherty, a licensed psychologist in Portland, Ore., who takes an environmental approach to mental health. "It looks troubling; it feels troubling," Doherty says, "the smell, the haze."

As wildfire season wears on, many more people may end up under a smoky haze, making it important to be aware of the potential mental health fallout, even for those far from the flames. While researchers have long known that wildfire smoke affects physical health, studies are increasingly suggesting that exposure to fires and smoke also affect mental health. Research indicates that losing property or having to flee a nearby wildfire can cause lingering symptoms of depression, anxiety and post-traumatic stress, even years later. The impact of smoke exposure alone is less well studied, but some emerging research suggests it is linked to lower standardized test scores in schoolchildren. Meanwhile studies on air pollution more broadly suggest that people who breathe bad air have higher rates of anxiety and depression. More immediately, facing wildfire smoke for the first time can cause a spike in stress, Doherty says.

"It's normal to feel overwhelmed," he says. "It's a lot to take on."

Facing Down Fire

Living through a wildfire in one's own community can have long-lasting mental health consequences, even for those who didn't lose loved ones or property. A review of research published in 2021 in *Behavioral Sciences* found elevated rates of post-traumatic stress disorder (PTSD) up to 10 years later in communities damaged by fires. Depression symptoms were also elevated a decade later. Anxiety is less studied, but preliminary research suggests that both adults and children who experience wildfires have higher rates of anxiety and panic disorders in the months after.

The trauma of these natural disasters can also lead to long-lasting cognitive effects, says Jyoti Mishra, a neuroscientist at the University of California, San Diego. Mishra's work has found that people who experienced California's devastating Camp Fire of 2018 showed a decreased ability to concentrate and to ignore distractions, compared with people who weren't exposed. Her team recorded these symptoms in people six to 12 months after the fire. The results, published in January in *PLOS Climate*, also showed that people who had been directly impacted by the fire, such as by losing property or having to flee flames, and those who simply witnessed the fires in their community both experienced similar cognitive impairments.

"These fire-impacted populations can have greater PTSD symptoms, anxiety and depression, so it's a complex set of mental health systems that develop," Mishra says. Mental health conditions are known to influence cognitive processing, she adds. For example, PTSD puts the brain in a constant state of hyperalertness, which makes it harder to filter out distracting information.

Surviving any natural disaster can also have long-term impacts on education and income, says Jisung Park, who researches how environmental factors impact economic opportunities at the University of Pennsylvania. In a study published on June 1 in *Nature Human Behavior*, Park and his colleagues found that residents of communities who had survived a natural disaster, such as hurricanes or floods, saw their lifetime educational attainment and earnings decline. "A disaster that causes $100 per person in physical damages appears to reduce human capital by roughly the same magnitude," as measured by the predicted future earnings loss for individuals, Park says. (Human capital is an economics term for the knowledge, skills and health that enable people's productivity.) Though Park and his team did not study mental health outcomes, education and earnings can have their own impacts on mental health—for example, someone with less financial security might experience more stress. Disasters may also exacerbate existing financial and health inequalities, Park says.

Coping with Smoke

There are few studies on the health impacts of wildfire smoke specifically, but smoke contains many of the same particulates and contaminates as air pollution. Research on air pollution has been consistent. For example, breathing polluted air lowers test scores in school-age children. A small but similar trend is seen in wildfire smoke: a 2022 study published in *Nature Sustainability* found that wildfire smoke exposure during the school year lowered standardized test scores slightly, compared with years without any smoke exposure.

Air pollution also makes people feel mentally worse. In one large study in China, university students exposed to worse air had lower levels of happiness and higher levels of depression, compared with those exposed to less air pollution. Another review study in 2022 found not only elevated symptoms of depression and anxiety linked to air pollution but also functional and structural changes in multiple brain areas.

In only a handful of studies have researchers tried to investigate the link between exposure to wildfire smoke and mental health, and the results have been mixed. One 2014 paper, published in *BMC Psychiatry*, showed that after a massive wildfire smoke event in Southeast Asia, locals reported mild psychological stress, which was worst in those who had a higher number of physical symptoms from the smoke and those who perceived the air quality to be dangerous (which it likely was for many). A 2011 study in *Environmental Health* found an uptick in the use of anxiety drugs and sedatives after wildfires in northwest Spain, but researchers did not query people directly about mental health. Meanwhile a pair of older studies—one on people who experienced smoke from 2003 wildfires in British Columbia and another on people affected by smoke from 1987 fires in California—found no increase in mental-health-related doctor visits or hospitalizations.

Psychologists, however, are increasingly reporting that their patients are reacting to natural disasters with feelings of grief and loss. This could be caused in part by an increasing number of wildfires affecting populated areas as the climate warms and dries or increasing public awareness that these events herald future climate crises, or some combination of both. "Climate change is a mental health issue," says Nancy Piotrowski, a licensed psychologist in Vallejo, Calif., and council representative for the American Psychological Association's Society for Environmental, Population and Conservation Psychology.

Given the warming, drying climate, smoke events trigger worries about the future. Piotrowski says her patients often wonder, "Will this happen again? How often?" and "Will next time be worse?" But she adds that not all anxiety is bad. "Anxiety helps get us prepared when we have to get ready to take action," she says. "But we don't want it to be paralyzing."

To cope with the stress of a smoke event, Piotrowski recommends preparedness, including knowing where to look for air quality information and keeping a stash of N95 or KN95 masks, which are effective at blocking smoke particulates. Getting involved in advocacy around climate or other environmental issues can also help a person feel more informed and contribute to solutions that make communities safer from wildfire, she says. If the anxiety becomes overwhelming, she says, don't dismiss it. A psychologist or other mental health professional can help with coping tools. Cognitive-behavioral therapy, for example, has proved effective at treating anxiety by training people to overcome distorted thinking and use problem-solving techniques to cope with challenges.

"It is not something to dismiss as small. It is a major disruption to people's lives," Doherty agrees. He and other psychologists in the Climate Psychology Alliance, an organization of mental health professionals concerned about the emotional fallout of climate change, are working to raise awareness of ecoanxiety and trying to get terms such as "climate grief" into popular therapist databases such as the *Psychology Today* directory so that people can more readily find support.

"I think the wildfires of this month will be yet another tipping point in our public consciousness of climate change," Doherty says.

About the Author

Stephanie Pappas is a freelance science journalist based in Denver, Colo.

How Wildfires Kill People

By Tanya Lewis

The devastating wildfires on Hawaii's island of Maui this month, including one that ripped through the historic town of Lahaina and razed much of its iconic Front Street to the ground, have killed at least 97 people. The blaze in Lahaina is now the deadliest wildfire in the U.S. in more than a century. At a news conference on August 10, Hawaii's governor Josh Green compared the destruction in Lahaina to a bomb going off. The fast-moving flames, which were fueled by dry conditions and high winds, caught a lot of people completely unaware. Many fled by car or even jumped into the ocean, where some were rescued by the Coast Guard; others were not so lucky.

In such deadly blazes, smoke inhalation is the most common cause of death: people inhale carbon monoxide and other gases and fine particles that make it hard to breathe. People can also die from building damage, and some die directly from burns. The air pollution from wildfires also has long-term health effects for survivors, including asthma and other diseases. And climate change is making the conditions that lead to such deadly fires more frequent around the world.

Scientific American spoke with Vanessa Kerry, the World Health Organization's special envoy for climate change and health and CEO of Seed Global Health, about the ways that wildfires kill and the need to take action to prevent and prepare for them.

[An edited transcript of the interview follows.]

Q: What are the ways that fires can kill people directly?

A: There are a number of ways wildfires can kill. One is direct injury and burns if you are caught in a fire. Or when fires happen in urban places, you can get destruction of buildings. You can get explosions, as we've seen in Hawaii with gas stations blowing up and things like that, that can cause direct trauma and burns. Burns can be very deadly because they disrupt the skin barriers that you have and can create a host of problems and infections. But probably the biggest way and the most widespread one that we've experienced—whether it's been the wildfires on Maui, in Canada, in Europe or all around the world that are accelerating in rate—is smoke inhalation. It is the most common cause of death from fires.

Q: What is smoke inhalation, and why is it so deadly?

A: I'm a critical care physician and have had to deal very much directly with what inhalation injuries can look like. It's a mix of direct fine particles from burning vegetation, but [there] also can be volatile compounds from building materials and other materials. So it's a mix of gases and fine particles that can cause direct injury to the body. If your body can't clear it, it can cause direct inflammation of the linings of your lungs, which can slough off and make it hard to breathe and require breathing support.

Q: Do you know what might have caused the fatalities in the fire in Lahaina?

A: I don't know. I think that in any fire, some of it is obviously direct death—getting caught in a fire itself. From what I understand, because of Hurricane Dora [which passed south of Hawaii], the winds were really strong..., and also it's very dry, so these fires are moving incredibly quickly. So the combination of smoke inhalation and possibly direct burns would be the most likely, but I can't report on that entirely, other than just what the risks are and the scope and scale and severity and rate that this is happening.

Q: What are the long-term health risks of wildfire smoke?

A: For those who aren't directly exposed but have the kind of secondary exposures like we saw [with the June wildfire smoke in] New York City, you can have asthma attacks and increases in cardiovascular events and strokes. There's the mental health distress of what happens. I think that what people don't also realize is that our economy shut down. Our worlds tend to stop when we have these large fires. And that can be a loss of income, which can be a loss of access to health for people, so there's a whole cascade here.

It's important to realize that the fires we're seeing in Maui, as devastating as they are, are just one of a multitude of fires and risks that we're seeing now at the intersection of accelerating extreme weather events, extreme heat and climate [change]. And unfortunately, air pollution is already killing one person every five seconds, which amounts to about seven million people a year. That's more than [the number of people that] died in the entire COVID pandemic over the course of three years.

Q: What role does climate change play in these kinds of wildfires?

A: We're seeing changes in rainfall and changes in weather patterns that are making droughts more common, which is basically creating a tinderbox for these fires to spread—and to spread rapidly and quickly. When you combine this with severe weather events happening around the world, such as a hurricane that is hundreds of miles offshore, it creates a deadly combination that is directly killing Americans. And we see in other places around the world that it's killing around the globe.

Q: How common is it for there to be direct fatalities like there were in Lahaina?

A: I don't know the statistic off the top of my head, but you can imagine it has to do with the urban density and the speed and the severity of the fires. What I can tell you is: we're going to be seeing more and more fatalities from [such events]. The World Health Organization has an estimate that there are going to be an additional 250,000 deaths a year from climate change and the impacts of climate change on human health. That's on top of the fact that one in four deaths is already from a preventable environmental cause today—and wildfires fall in that category. We're crossing tipping points every day. And climate experts are saying we are in completely uncharted territory.

Q: If someone is in a threatening wildfire situation, what are the most important things they can do to protect themselves?

A: I think just use common sense. If you find yourself in a wildfire situation, [don't] hunker down. I would evacuate, and I would find out where safety is. [Don't stop] to save all your most precious things.... Be thoughtful about getting out quickly. These fires do go very rapidly, especially with winds, and you can get caught in really bad situations. I think that's why we've seen the death toll in Maui be what it is and why people fled into the ocean.

Q: What can we do as a society to prevent and prepare for these disasters?

A: We can start to demand real action and change right now. We are not on track to meet the Paris [climate accord] goals. We are still increasing the greenhouse gas emissions in the world. And we can change that. This is a choice we make—our leaders make. And we can choose who our leaders are, [the people] who are going to actually protect our health and well-being. So as we are watching our homes burn, our livelihoods get consumed by climate change, we need to demand a different kind of action.

The other thing we can do is start to really invest in strong health systems that can actually adapt and be resilient in these moments. The hospitals on Maui are overwhelmed right now. And that speaks to the fact that we're not anticipating the health burdens and the outcomes that we're going to see from this change that are already happening. So we have to start investing in stronger health systems; we have to start investing in a workforce that is available and trained in what these climate emergencies are going to look like and that is at the ready. And we need to be able to really prioritize the things that are going to keep us healthy and safe in a way that we haven't before.

About the Author

Tanya Lewis is a senior editor covering health and medicine at Scientific American. *She writes and edits stories for the website and print magazine on topics ranging from COVID to organ transplants. She also appears on* Scientific American's *podcast* Science, Quickly *and writes* Scientific American's *weekly Health & Biology newsletter. She has held a number of positions over her eight years at Scientific American, including health editor, assistant news editor and associate editor at* Scientific American Mind. *Previously, she has written for outlets that include* Insider, Wired, Science News, *and others. She has a degree in biomedical engineering from Brown University and one in science communication from the University of California, Santa Cruz. Follow her on Bluesky @tanyalewis.bsky.social.*

Hurricanes Kill People for Years after the Initial Disaster

By Andrea Thompson

More than 160 people have lost their lives to the ferocious winds and catastrophic flooding wrought by Hurricane Helene. But the true death toll will take years—likely more than a decade—to unfold.

A new study published on Wednesday in *Nature* found that the average tropical cyclone in the U.S. ultimately causes about 7,000 to 11,000 excess deaths (those beyond what would typically be expected), compared with the average of 24 direct deaths reported in official statistics. The study's authors estimated that, between 1950 and 2015, tropical storms and hurricanes caused between 3.6 million and 5.2 million excess deaths—more than those caused by traffic deaths or infectious diseases. And such storm-related deaths involve people from some groups more than others, marking an "important and understudied contributor to health in the United States, particularly for young or Black populations," the authors wrote.

"These are individuals who are dying years before they would have otherwise," says study co-author Rachel Young, an environmental economist at the University of California, Berkeley.

This study is part of a burgeoning trend: assessing the full health consequences of the growing number of disasters fueled by climate change. Epidemiologists and other experts have increasingly been emphasizing that heat wave deaths are significantly underestimated, and recent research has found that wildfire smoke kills thousands of people in California—many more than the actual flames. "We thought that there was something similar with hurricanes," Young says.

So she and Stanford University economist Solomon Hsiang looked at hurricanes that hit the U.S. from 1930 to 2015, as well as mortality data and used statistical methods to compare a state's deaths before a storm with those that occurred over the course of

20 years after—from 1950 to 2015. "We thought we'd see maybe six months or a year of a delayed effect," Young says, but data showed excess deaths occurring for 15 years after a storm. "We were so stunned," she says, that the researchers spent years testing and retesting to make sure the effect was real.

Thinking beyond the data, the duration of the effect makes sense because "these are huge events," Young says. "Look at what's going on with Helene." Families may have to spend months in damaged or mold-riddled homes before repairs are made. People may have to use their savings for repairs, leaving less money for their health care for years. People may be forced to move and live farther away from crucial social support networks. And these events exert a considerable mental health burden. "It's devastating to the individuals, and it's devastating to the local and state governments, too," Young says, noting that other research shows these governments experience budget declines for many years after a hurricane. For those affected, she adds, "you're in a version of the world where you have less money, you have less resources, you have more pollution exposure"—a bad combination when it comes to staying healthy.

When breaking out the data by age groups, the study found that people aged 65 and older had the largest number of storm-related excess deaths. But when the higher general probability of death in this age range was factored in, this group's storm death risk was smaller than that of others. The biggest risk was found to be for infants under the age of one, with almost all of these deaths occurring within less than two years after a storm. Young says that this effect could be influenced by people's inability to afford prenatal care in a storm's wake, as well as stress or other factors.

The risk of death was also higher among Black people than it was among white people, even though the white population that was exposed to storms was much larger than the exposed Black population.

The analysis further showed that "the mortality response isn't going down over time," Young says, meaning storms today have the same long-tail mortality impact as they did decades ago. Young and

Hsiang don't know exactly why this is the case and say it will take more research to dig into the reasons.

That mortality finding particularly struck Eugenio Paglino, a postdoctoral researcher at the Helsinki Institute of Demography and Population Health, who was not involved with the new study. He says that on first reading the paper's abstract, he thought the numbers of excess deaths the authors found "seemed pretty large," but he felt they did a thorough job of checking the robustness of the results. He would like to see additional research examine what might actually be causing these excess deaths and further bolster the findings.

Young and Hsiang also want to see this kind of follow-up research—and hope to do some themselves. It's a necessary step toward the ultimate goal of informing policymakers of what is needed to safeguard communities in the face of the growing climate disaster. As Helene shows, "local and state governments and first responders are doing heroic work to help people after disasters," Young says. "We don't want their efforts to be in vain."

About the Author

Andrea Thompson is an associate editor covering the environment, energy and earth sciences. She has been covering these issues for 16 years. Prior to joining Scientific American, *she was a senior writer covering climate science at* Climate Central *and a reporter and editor at* Live Science, *where she primarily covered earth science and the environment. She has moderated panels, including as part of the United Nations Sustainable Development Media Zone, and appeared in radio and television interviews on major networks. She holds a graduate degree in science, health and environmental reporting from New York University, as well as a B.S. and an M.S. in atmospheric chemistry from the Georgia Institute of Technology. Follow Thompson on Bluesky @andreatweather.bsky.social.*

What's in Floodwaters?

By Meghan Bartles

When large storms or hurricanes inundate areas with a storm surge and torrential rain, the resulting floodwaters pose major risks beyond the immediate physical damage they cause. As water accumulates in a region, whether the cause is a storm's effects, a dam failure or any other reason, it picks up a host of threats to human health, including bacteria, viruses, chemicals, debris, downed power lines and even wild animals.

And those threats are only increasing as climate change causes floods to become more frequent around the world. "Flooding is going to continue to be an increasingly common problem," says Thomas Frazer, an ecologist at the University of South Florida, who studies flooding. "We're faced with a reality of rising sea levels, more intense tropical storms and hurricanes and just extreme rainfall events more generally."

The smallest materials in floodwaters can be the most dangerous, says Henry Briceño, a Florida International University geologist who studies water. "The problems are things that, many of them, you don't see," he says, citing in particular the pathogens and chemicals that can accumulate in floodwaters.

Pathogens often come from overwhelmed water-management systems that trigger sewage outflows—although bacteria such as the "flesh-eating," wound-infecting *Vibrio* species can also ride in from the wild on seawater. "You might flood a septic system; you might have a sewage spill," Frazer says. "So there's a high likelihood that you're going to get a lot of contaminants, pathogens potentially, into the water."

Whether a flooded area is urban or rural, the waters can also pick up a range of chemicals usually kept safely away from humans, such as motor oil and cleaning chemicals from cities or pesticides and fertilizers from agricultural lands.

Other threats are physically larger. Downed power lines can electrify floodwaters, and tree limbs and other wreckage can hurt people trying to move through water, particularly if that wreckage is below the surface. "You often can't see it, and it can be moving rapidly," Frazer says.

Floodwaters can also carry wildlife. In Florida that can include examples as dramatic as alligators. More commonly floods displace animals such as snakes and rats—or prompt fire ants to form escape "rafts," floating masses of the painfully stinging insects.

The basic mix of threats present in floodwater is the same around the world, Frazer and Briceño say, although the exact soup can vary depending on local conditions. In some areas of Africa, South Asia and the Caribbean, for example, floods have been known to spread the bacteria that cause the diarrheal disease cholera.

Taken together, it's no surprise that emergency personnel recommend that you should stay out of floodwaters whenever possible, even if you're in a vehicle. But while it's best to avoid contact with floodwater, that's not always feasible for people who need to evacuate an area during an emergency and its aftermath—or for rescuers who try to help them. Still, experts warn those dealing with flooding not to underestimate the dangers of this water.

"You don't ever want to ingest floodwaters," Frazer says. "Definitely try to take a shower, bath, whatever you need to do as soon as possible. You just want to reduce the exposure to pathogens and toxins that might be in that water; you want to get them off your body." If at all possible, it's best to keep any injuries high and dry. "Be careful with scratches and things like that," Briceño says, "because those are places for bacteria and pathogens to enter your body."

When floodwater lingers, particularly in warmer regions, it can also become a breeding ground for both pathogens and mosquitos that can carry them, Frazer says—so people in flooded areas shouldn't lower their guard as time passes.

And even for people who live far from coasts, it's important to remember that flooding can occur anywhere. "Flooding comes in all forms—it's not just restricted to our coastal areas. We see it inland, in low-elevation areas as well as high-elevation areas," Frazer says. "The general problem is geographically agnostic."

About the Author

Meghan Bartels is a science journalist based in New York City. She joined Scientific American *in 2023 and is now a senior news reporter there. Previously, she spent more than four years as a writer and editor at* Space.com, *as well as nearly a year as a science reporter at* Newsweek, *where she focused on space and Earth science. Her writing has also appeared in* Audubon, Nautilus, Astronomy *and* Smithsonian, *among other publications. She attended Georgetown University and earned a master's degree in journalism at New York University's Science, Health and Environmental Reporting Program.*

Section 4: What We Consume

How a Chemist and His 'Poison Squad' Inspired the First Food Safety Regulations

By Tanya Lewis

I t was common in the 1800s for people to consume milk containing formaldehyde, meat preserved with salicylic acid and borax, and "coffee" filled with ground up bones and charred lead.

The 19th century was largely unregulated, especially when it came to food. "Medical historians always call that period the century of the great American stomachache," says Deborah Blum, a Pulitzer Prize–winning science journalist and author of the 2018 book *The Poison Squad: One Chemist's Single-Minded Crusade for Food Safety at the Turn of the Twentieth Century.*

Food adulteration and the use of harmful ingredients were not even illegal because there were no laws around food safety or purity in the U.S. It wasn't until 1883 that a former Purdue University chemist, who had just become chief chemist of the U.S. Department of Agriculture, started investigating fraud involving foods and drinks: Harvey Washington Wiley and a small group of his colleagues experimented on young men who became known as the "poison squad." The researchers exposed these men to various questionable foods and observed the effects. Wiley's methods were somewhat unorthodox—by modern standards, perhaps unethical—but it was the first attempt to gather data for any sort of regulation of an industry that was sickening and killing many people.

Others aided the crusade for better food safety, including journalist and activist Upton Sinclair, author of the 1905 novel *The Jungle*, which famously exposed the horrific practices of the U.S. meat industry; food manufacturer Henry Heinz; and cookbook author Fannie Farmer. As a result of these efforts, in 1906 Congress finally passed the Federal Meat Inspection Act and the Pure Food and Drug Act, the latter of which became known as the "Wiley Act" and

"Dr. Wiley's law." These laws contained strict regulations over the conditions under which meat was produced and eventually laid the groundwork for the creation of the Food and Drug Administration. The laws were not perfect, however, and there have been several attempts to refine these regulatory powers over the decades since.

Today the food industry continues to push back against federal regulation. Recently U.S. congressional representatives introduced the Food Traceability Enhancement Act, which would exempt food retailers from many of the rules the FDA uses to track outbreaks of foodborne illness. If the act passes, it could significantly impede the FDA's ability to find the source of such outbreaks, which can be deadly.

Scientific American spoke with Blum about the history of food safety in the U.S. and the way that history continues to inform our relationship with food regulation today.

[An edited transcript of the interview follows.]

Q: What was the status of food safety in the 19th century?

A: The U.S. was really slow to the food safety game. There were regulations in Europe and in Canada before we actually took this up. There was just an incredible amount of 19th-century U.S. resistance to the idea of the federal government, as someone said, becoming the "policeman" of your stomach. And so that whole American ethos of "nobody tells me what to do," individual rights, all of those things really played into it, as well as enormous industry resistance.

Q: Then along came Harvey Washington Wiley. How did he launch federal oversight of food in this country?

A: I describe him as a "crusading chemist"—I sometimes call him a "Holy Roller chemist"—who was absolutely passionate about the idea that we needed to do something to make the American food supply safer. He had been the first professor of chemistry at Purdue University at a time when it only had six faculty members, including the university's president. He had studied deceptive food practices when he was in Indiana. And when he came to the federal government, he was head of what was then called the Bureau of Chemistry at the USDA. He launched the federal government, for the first time in its history, into looking at the idea of food safety and food integrity. There were people who did it at the state level, but at the national level, there was no scientist looking at it.

In 1883, when my guy Wiley arrives at the USDA, there are fewer than a dozen chemists at the agency. They're responsible for all the agricultural chemistry issues in the U.S.—everything from pesticides to crop growth to soil quality. He tells them, Now we're going to test the integrity of the American food supply. And they do it! Starting in the 1880s, this tiny group of chemists starts doing a series of reports that have the very boring title of "Bulletin 13." And the chemists look at dairy, and they look at canned vegetables, and they look at coffee and tea, and they look at wine and beer and spices and processed meats. And they really take apart the processed, industrialized food system of the U.S. And across the board, they find really, really bad things.

Q: What were some examples of the questionable food practices they found?

A: Some of it was just fraud. There was, like, 90 percent adulteration of spices. If you were buying cinnamon, you were buying brick dust. If you were buying pepper, you were buying dirt or charred and ground rope. If you were buying coffee, sometimes you were just buying ground shells. People would grind up bones and charred lead into coffee. If you got flour, you got gypsum. If you got milk, you got chalk or plaster of paris. And actual milk was full of horrible bacteria—there was no pasteurization; there was no refrigeration. People started putting preservatives such as formaldehyde in milk; the milk started killing people around the country. All of this was completely legal. No one could ever be prosecuted for any of this.

Q: That's pretty horrifying. What motivated Wiley to take action?

A: There's no requirement to honestly label anything [at this time]. So you see Wiley starting to say, There are so many of these additives in food, such as formaldehyde and salicylic acid, which causes the lining of your stomach to bleed, and all these other things. Why can't we just tell people what's in the food so they know how many times a day they're eating these products? There's absolute industry resistance to this. Nothing passes. Wiley goes to Congress. Nothing happens. In the entire 19th century, [hardly any] federal regulation regarding food safety or drink safety or drug safety gets through Congress, which is pretty much owned by industry at this point.

Q: So what did Wiley do about it?

A: Wiley ran what the *Washington Post* called these "poison squad" experiments, in which he experimented with young workers at the USDA and put these different additives in their food and poisoned them, essentially. The whole science of epidemiology, the science of public health, is so in its infancy at this point. His poison squad experiments had a control group—he had two groups that all consumed the same foods and drinks, but one group got these additives, and one of them didn't. It's super primitive to us today, but it was really forward-looking and kind of methodical. It was a completely illegal experiment by today's standards; they'd be, like, running you out of town now.

Q: But it wasn't just Wiley and his poison squad, right? Weren't there other people crusading for the cause of food safety at that time?

A: You have what was called the pure food movement. Wiley did a lot of talking to women's groups. Women couldn't vote at that time, but he thought they were very politically organized and powerful. So he went and worked with a lot of women's groups who crusaded for the cause. He found some friendly manufacturers such as [Ketchup entrepreneur] Henry J. Heinz. And there's this start of a push toward at least public recognition that food is unsafe. In the cookbooks of the time, you have cookbook writers such as Fannie Farmer saying, Okay, I'm going to tell you to put coffee in this recipe—just be aware that it's not going to be coffee, or, You should not put milk in the food of sick people because it's so dangerous.

Upton Sinclair, a socialist writer, writes this book, *The Jungle*. It was first published in the socialist newspaper *Appeal to Reason* as a call to arms about the plight of the worker. And he finally gets a New York City publisher to agree to publish it. Because he had gone and embedded himself in the stockyards of Chicago, he has all this incredible description about how horrible meat processing is and the mold that's growing on the meat that still goes into the potted ham and the disease and the rotting animals that go into the sausage. The publisher sends fact-checkers to Chicago to make sure that this isn't all just bullshit, and the fact-checkers come back, and they say, It's even worse than he says. A copy was sent to President Theodore Roosevelt. The book becomes this big explosion. Nobody cares about the plight of the worker. There's that famous quote from Upton Sinclair, "I aimed for the public's heart, and by accident I hit it in the stomach."

Q: So what did Roosevelt do about the situation? How did it lead to Congress passing food safety regulations?

A: There's such a storm about *The Jungle* that Roosevelt sends his own fact-checkers to Chicago. And the crazy thing about that visit is that the meat-packers know they're coming. The meat-packers clean up the stockyards. And these fact-checkers come back, and they also go, "It's even worse than in the book." Roosevelt then goes to Congress, which is entirely in the pocket of the meat industry, and says, I want a meat inspection act. If you don't give me a meat inspection act, I'm going to publish this report.

He ends up publishing about six to eight pages of this report, which was almost 100 pages. Those six pages are so explosive that every country in Europe cancels its meat contract with the

U.S.. And at that point, the packing industry goes, Oh, my God, we're going to have to have a meat inspection act. And so the Federal Meat Inspection Act goes through Congress.

Q: What did the Federal Meat Inspection Act do?

A: The act has got a ton of teeth in it. The meat industry has to actually pay to help inspect the meat; the meat inspectors have real power in the factories. It's got a lot of funding built in. There's a powerful recall apparatus built into the meat inspection act. And in this kind of storm of legislative outrage over the food supply, the Pure Food and Drug Act passes, but because it has been a political football for 20 years, it's a mess, and there's not a good funding apparatus. It's got a lot of problems in terms of how you actually measure and enforce toxic substances in food, and that difference haunts our regulatory system today.

Even today, under the Federal Meat Inspection Act, the USDA inspects meat-processing factories. It inspects about 10 to 20 percent of the food processing in the U.S., and it has almost the exact same budget that the FDA gets to inspect the other 80 percent of food. And a legacy of the difference between those two acts persists—one act was driven by a huge scandal that was incredibly powerful and had the backing of industry, and one was dragged over the line with industry hostile to it, working almost from the beginning to undo all of its better applications.

Q: Bring us back to the present. How does the legacy of these food regulation laws continue to affect us today?

A: The Pure Food and Drug Act was eventually replaced by the 1938 Food, Drug, and Cosmetic Act, which created the modern FDA. There have been multiple [attempted] amendments since then to the FDA's power, such as the Food Traceability Enhancement Act. But the fundamental weakness of the powers of the FDA to enforce safety measures in food, drugs and cosmetics—that still underlies our system in terms of both funding and in terms of some of the enforcement mechanisms we see today.

To be fair, the Federal Meat Inspection Act and the Pure Food and Drug Act of 1906 were paradigm-shifting laws. It was the first time in U.S. history that the government said, Yes, we're in the business of protecting consumers. All of the consumer-protective things that followed—the Occupational Safety and Health Administration, the Environmental Protection Agency, the modern FDA—all of those agencies are built on those two laws. I mean, they made a huge and important difference.

Q: So, despite industry pushback, all of these government regulations of our food supply have made Americans safer.
A: There's no borax or salicylic acid added to our wine and beer. We're not using arsenic as green food coloring. We're not using red lead to make cheddar cheese look a little more orange.

If I could persuade people not to think of regulation as a pejorative term, my life's work would be done.

About the Author

Tanya Lewis is a senior editor covering health and medicine at Scientific American. *She writes and edits stories for the website and print magazine on topics ranging from COVID to organ transplants. She also appears on* Scientific American's *podcast* Science, Quickly *and writes* Scientific American's *weekly Health & Biology newsletter. She has held a number of positions over her eight years at* Scientific American, *including health editor, assistant news editor and associate editor at* Scientific American Mind. *Previously, she has written for outlets that include* Insider, Wired, Science News, *and others. She has a degree in biomedical engineering from Brown University and one in science communication from the University of California, Santa Cruz. Follow her on Bluesky @tanyalewis. bsky.social.*

The FDA Is Changing What Foods Can Be Called 'Healthy'

By Reyna Gobel

U ntil now, an orange couldn't be called healthy, according to U.S. Food and Drug Administration. The fruit has 70 calories, three grams of fiber and more than 100 percent of the recommended daily value for vitamin C. Yet the whole fruit can't qualify for a "healthy" label based on existing FDA guidelines for use of the term. Water can't do so either—along with pistachios, bananas and many other fresh foods.

But what's labeled "healthy" is about to change. A revised FDA rule, just announced this month, would allow whole foods such as oranges, in addition to fish such as salmon, to qualify as healthy. What can no longer use the word? Foods that have higher amounts of added sugar or saturated fats than the rule allows.

This change—the first in 30 years—could stop a lot of companies that call their breakfast cereals "healthy" from using the word on the box. The agency is working on a logo symbolizing "healthy" that manufacturers can use only if they meet new standards, but that may take a while.

The old rule for using the word healthy on a food label was that the grocery item must contribute at least 10 percent of the established daily value of certain vitamins, calcium, iron, protein or fiber and not go over specific limits for saturated fat, total fat, sodium or cholesterol. The nutrients didn't have to occur in the product naturally.

"The current rule is dangerously outdated, focusing on 1980 dietary priorities around fat and saturated fat, and so on," says Dariush Mozaffarian, a cardiologist and director of the Food Is Medicine Institute at the Friedman School of Nutrition Science and Policy at Tufts University. He says the rule needed to change to focus on the FDA's 2020–2025 Dietary Guidelines recommendations, which no longer accept adding nutrients in most foods as a replacement for a naturally occurring nutrient. Thus, an orange that has 100 percent of the recommended daily value of natural vitamin C is now preferred to most orange juices, which drain the nutrient-rich pulp from the juice, in a healthy diet.

The revised rule for adding healthy labels promotes eating whole foods—foods that have not gone through a process that could remove nutrients such as fiber—and also low-sugar and low-saturated-fat foods that include enough protein, oil, grains, vegetables or fruit by volume.

The previous rule did not require a product to be low in added sugar to be labeled healthy. But the new rule does. For instance, a food that meets the standards for protein—meat, seafood, beans, eggs, nuts or seeds—can't have more than two percent of the recommended daily amount of sugar. This automatically eliminates, for example, chicken sausage with maple that may be otherwise healthy. Vegetable and fruit products must have no added sugar, and dairy and grain products can have up to five percent of the recommended daily value. Saturated fat content also is subject to sharp limits: five or 10 percent of the daily value depending on the type of protein.

Why did the FDA choose to limit added sugar? The agency consulted the *Scientific Report of the 2020 Dietary Guidelines Advisory Committee*, the same report that the Dietary Guidelines for Americans are based on. A scientific committee analyzed 23 studies, and found that added sugar could increase overall caloric intake without a nutritional benefit like the ones you would get from a vegetable or whole grain.

The 2013–2016 data from the National Health and Nutrition Examination Survey (NHANES) that influenced the report showed that the average added sugar consumption contributed at least 200 calories to daily diets across all age and sex groups. At the same time, most people did not eat in a way that met food group and nutrient requirements.

Food companies object to the sugar standards, however, and argue they could actually induce consumers to buy products with more fat. Sarah Gallo, senior vice president of product policy and federal affairs at the Consumer Brands Association, which represents most companies selling packaged foods, says that if foods currently able to describe themselves as "healthy" are barred from using the word because of sugar content, "consumers may migrate to full-flavor offerings that contain more saturated fat, added sugars and sodium." In other words, why get one lasagna over another if the fuller-fat one doesn't have a healthy label either?

Gallo adds that "the FDA's proposed added sugars limit may reflect an inaccurate understanding of the products available in the marketplace and how truly restrictive FDA's proposed added sugars thresholds are."

Indeed, very few cereals and yogurts that you see on grocery shelves meet the added sugar limits. After reviewing a draft version of the new rule, the Consumer Brands Association noted in response that one of its member companies applied the FDA's proposed criteria to its 195 yogurt products and 104 cereals. Only three cereals and 24 yogurts had sugar levels that qualified as healthy.

Nutrition experts are more optimistic about the new standards, because the "healthy" label offers people an easy way to find some healthy foods. "I can tell my patients that foods with a healthy label are a safe bet. It takes time, 15 to 20 minutes, [to] learn how to read a nutrition label," and not everyone will take the time, says Courtney Pelitera, a registered dietitian specializing in sports nutrition and wellness nutrition. "Any shortcuts are helpful."

Unfortunately, the label leaves no room for foods that may not go all the way to meeting the standards but come close. For instance, a Trader Joe's Chicken Burrito Bowl has 22 grams of protein, nine grams of fiber and three kinds of whole grains. It seems like a nutritionally solid choice among frozen food options for nutrients and balance among food groups. In part because it uses full-fat cheddar cheese, however, it has 4.5 grams of saturated fat, or 23 percent of the total recommended daily value. That is slightly above the 20 percent (four-gram) recommended daily value required to qualify as healthy. Someone who has a meal within that limit could easily make up for the 0.5 gram extra of saturated fat by eating a low-fat cheese or yogurt in another meal. And even if all three of their meals that day had 23 percent of the recommended daily value, that would still be under the daily total; they could get up to 31 percent of their daily value of saturated fat from snacks and still meet the guideline.

Consumer brands are finding other ways to show consumers which options are healthier than others, Gallo says. It's not unusual to see a package advertise the number of grams of whole grains a product has or the lack of added sugar, even though it might not meet the healthy label. Front-of-package labels often show fiber, protein, saturated fats, and so on. "I can tell my patients to look for certain saturated fat, fiber and protein numbers on labels," Pelitera says.

While Mozaffarian supports the new healthy label requirements, he recommends the FDA take a different approach to encourage products to change to healthier recipes. "Imagine a front-of-package label that showed the actual servings of fruits, vegetables, whole grains, beans and legumes and nuts and seeds in a package," he says. That would give companies an incentive to start to increase those ingredients.

Another option is a graded system, and the Food Is Medicine Institute is testing one. "We've done a randomized control trial for our Food Compass label, which is our more graded system that goes from 1 to 100" to rate how healthy a food is, Mozaffarian says. While the results aren't published yet, he says, "we found that the Food Compass works even better [for] most people to [make] healthier shopping decisions."

There is an overarching question about the new FDA rule: Will it pass muster with the incoming Trump administration, which has professed antipathy toward certain regulations? Some experts in food policy think it will be fine. "I don't see the next administration fighting it. It's a voluntary label claim," says David Joy, a partner of international regulatory law firm Keller and Heckman, who worked for 15 years in the Office of Regulatory Policy in the FDA's Center for Drug Evaluation and Research. "FDA is updating the criteria for 'healthy' claims on food labels in line with current dietary guidelines, and this isn't a big regulatory burden for the food industry," he says.

But Emily Lyons, a food regulatory attorney and partner of the law firm Husch Blackwell, believes the Trump administration might make changes because the food industry does have concerns with parts of the rule. She also notes that Robert F. Kennedy Jr., Trump's choice to run the Department of Health and Human Services, may want to make his own changes, such as banning certain food dyes. The FDA policy "could be subject to the Congressional Review Act, which means that when Republicans take control of both the House and Senate, they could potentially repeal it," Lyons says.

Even if the rule stands as written now, new labels could take at least two years to change on products in the grocery store. But if they do, people will be able to walk supermarket aisles and see that water, whole fruit, lean protein and a wider variety of whole grains are healthy to eat.

About the Author

Reyna Gobel is a freelance writer specializing in nutrition, with a master's degree in public health.

How Do Ultraprocessed Foods Affect Your Health?

By Lori Youmshajekian

Y ou might think you know a processed meal when you see one, but here's some food for thought: nearly every edible thing at the supermarket has undergone some kind of processing, such as washing, blanching, canning, drying or pasteurizing. In other words, if there is any change from the way the food begins to the way it ends up on a shelf, it counts as processed.

But then there are *ultraprocessed* foods. Both frozen chopped spinach and canned sausages are processed, but the latter have been through much more processing than the former. Ultraprocessed foods undergo an industrial process in their journey from farm to table. This often includes steps such as hydrogenation, which produces semisolid oils, and hydrolysis, which enhances flavors. These foods also contain a variety of additives that help to bind the ingredients together, increase their shelf life or make them more palatable.

According to some estimates, nearly 60 percent of the daily calories U.S. adults consume are from ultraprocessed foods. It's worse for kids and teenagers, whose diets are almost 70 percent ultraprocessed.

But a growing number of studies have linked higher consumption of ultraprocessed foods to a long list of health effects, and scientists are beginning to understand why.

What Are Ultraprocessed Foods?

Chicken nuggets, chips and hot dogs are considered ultraprocessed, but so are things such as fruit yogurts, mass produced bread and even some canned foods. As a rule of thumb, an ultraprocessed food is one that cannot be made in an ordinary kitchen—in other words, it contains at least one ingredient that is not typically found in homes or has undergone an industrial process that a home cook would not be able to replicate.

"A whole lot of things that you could never imagine can be done [to food]," says Barry Popkin, a professor of nutrition at the University of North Carolina at Chapel Hill. "You can't tell simply by the ingredients." For example, he says, "it'll be flour, but you really don't know that wheat flour has been decomposed in such complex ways and then put back together."

Researchers commonly use a four-part classification known as NOVA to group foods based on the extent of industrial processing they involve. The categories are unprocessed or minimally processed foods (which include vegetables and eggs), processed culinary ingredients (those that are usually added to food and rarely eaten alone, such as oils, butter and sugar), processed foods (those that are made from a combination of the first two groups, such as homemade bread), and ultraprocessed foods (those that are made with industrially modified raw ingredients and additives).

When NOVA was first introduced in 2009, it offered a new way of looking at food beyond its nutritional value. Take fortified breads or protein-rich cookies, for example: Compared with their unfortified equivalents, they would be considered relatively nutritious. But through the lens of NOVA, both are ultraprocessed.

Other researchers, such as Julie Hess, a nutritionist at the U.S. Department of Agriculture's Agricultural Research Service and former vice president of scientific affairs at the National Dairy Council, contend that NOVA is not the best or most consistent way to identify an ultraprocessed food. She argues that ultraprocessed foods are not all the same in terms of nutrition. "When we say 'ultraprocessed food,' are we going to include things like canned beans? Are we including canned oranges and dried peaches?" Hess asks. "That question of nutrient density isn't currently reflected in the NOVA categorization system."

Popkin and his colleagues looked at other ways to identify foods as ultraprocessed in an April 2024 paper. He says having at least one of 12 types of additives—including specific flavors, emulsifiers, foams, thickening agents and glazing agents—as an ingredient is a feature of all ultraprocessed foods. The presence of artificial coloring or flavoring would be a telltale sign for about 97 percent of these foods, he says.

Are Ultraprocessed Foods Bad for Your Health?

Many people believe that eating ultraprocessed food will make them gain weight or cause a host of other health issues, and some evidence backs this idea up. Research has tied the consumption of ultraprocessed foods to a slew of health conditions, including obesity, type 2 diabetes, some cancers, cardiovascular disease, and even mild depression and anxiety, but a clear mechanism for harm hasn't been identified.

A landmark paper in 2019 was the first to show a cause-and-effect link between ultraprocessed foods and weight gain. A group of 20 healthy volunteers was confined to a ward at the National Institutes of Health Clinical Center in Bethesda, Md., where the participants were randomly assigned to receive a diet of either ultraprocessed or minimally processed food for two weeks and then were switched to the other diet for the next two weeks. For example, a person receiving the ultraprocessed diet would start their day with foods such as packaged cereal and a blueberry muffin or croissants and turkey sausages. Someone eating the minimally processed diet would instead receive Greek yogurt and fruit or a fresh omelet and sweet potato hash.

On average, people eating the ultraprocessed diet consumed about 500 calories more per day, compared with those fed the minimally processed diet. Participants in the former group also ate faster and gained about two pounds after two weeks. On the minimally processed diet, participants ate less and lost about the same amount of weight as they gained on the processed diet. In both settings, participants were given access to about double the number of calories they needed and were told to eat as much as they wanted.

Kevin Hall, the study's lead author and a clinical researcher at the National Institute of Diabetes and Digestive and Kidney Diseases, says he designed the investigation because he thought the NOVA classification system—which doesn't account for the nutrients contained in different foods—was "nonsense." He matched foods in the two diets so that they had the same total amount of nutrients, including fat, carbohydrates and fiber, "because I thought the nutrients were going to drive the effects," Hall says. "And I was wrong."

Hess, who was not involved in the study, notes some limitations. There were "very, very different" foods in the two groups, she says—in other words, the study didn't match the diets for quality. Hall says the two diets used different foods because it would have been "very difficult to make homemade versions of many popular ultraprocessed foods while maintaining precise control over their nutrition content." Hess's lab designed a diet in which 90 percent of the calories were from ultraprocessed foods, and it still met most national guidelines for nutrients—calling into question how useful NOVA is for determining the healthfulness of a food when existing dietary guidelines are used as a benchmark.

Others say findings such as Hall's study suggest that processing may change how a food affects our body, independent of the nutrients that food contains. "It goes to show how much the [U.S. dietary] guidelines are focused on nutrients," says Filippa Juul, a nutritional epidemiologist at New York University. "You could have any food and just tune up the nutrients; it doesn't mean the food is necessarily healthy ... or has the same activity as nutrients that are in [unprocessed] foods."

Studies have also suggested a link between higher consumption of ultraprocessed foods and a profound change in the composition of gut microbes. And an altered gut microbiome has been linked to mental health conditions. The negative effects of these foods might also be a result of what they lack: fiber. The act of industrially processing a food can lower its fiber content, which can make it less filling. Fiber also feeds bacteria in the gut, and the absence of this nutrient may explain the links among diet, depression and gut health, too.

"There are probably some subcategories [of ultraprocessed foods] that are perfectly fine—maybe even really good for you—and others that are particularly damaging," Hall says. "I just don't think we know which ones [are which]." Part of the problem with ultraprocessed foods is that they're often packed with calories yet leave us craving more.

Why Do We Like Ultraprocessed Foods So Much?

Scientists still don't know for sure why humans gravitate toward ultraprocessed foods. One hypothesis, according to Hall, is that we might not be able to resist their combination of ingredients. Think about the last time you ate just one chip out of a bag—it's almost impossible not to eat more.

In a 2021 study, Hall attempted to compare a low-carbohydrate diet with a high-carbohydrate one to examine their effects on energy intake. When people were presented with meals that were high in both fat and sugar, fat and salt, or carbohydrates and salt, people tended to eat more calories, he says. "These are so-called hyperpalatable foods," Hall adds.

Such foods essentially have artificially enhanced palatability that exceeds the palatability any ingredient could produce on its own—in other words, they have a combination of fat, salt and sugar "that would never exist in nature," Juul says. Previous research showed that foods combining fat and carbohydrates were better at activating the brain's reward system than foods with just one of those ingredients. The ultraprocessed meals in Hall's study also had more calories per bite than the minimally processed foods.

Some researchers hypothesize that certain foods are addictive. People don't lose control over eating bananas, but with ultraprocessed foods, they show all the hallmarks of addiction, says Ashley Gearhardt, a professor of psychology at the University of Michigan. Addictive drugs activate the striatal dopamine system—the brain's pleasure center—by creating a dopamine spike followed by a rapid crash. "It's like a quick hit that isn't sustaining," Gearhardt observes. Ultraprocessed foods resemble nicotine and ethanol in the magnitude of that effect in the brain.

"That makes sense because the reward system of the brain was really shaped by the need to get calories," Gearhardt says. The addictive agent in food could be one of many things, she says, or some combination of them—taste, smell, sugar, fat and additives are all potential culprits. Studies in animals have shown that stopping the consumption of ultraprocessed foods elicits withdrawal symptoms such as anxiety and agitation, similar to what happens when people quit other addictive substances.

Should Ultraprocessed Food Be Regulated?

There are people who want to do away with ultraprocessed foods altogether and others who say there are not enough data to warrant any action, according to Hall. "It's not realistic to say, 'Well, we're just going to cut out 50 percent of the food,' " he says. "Who's going to make everybody's meals?" Ultraprocessed foods are a lot cheaper and more convenient than less processed ones, Hall says. In his study, the minimally processed meals cost 40 percent more to buy and took the chefs longer to prepare.

Spending hours hunched over a kitchen bench to churn butter is not the answer. But reducing consumption of ultraprocessed foods doesn't mean we have to make everything from scratch.

"There's an enormous number of things you can do," says Popkin, who eats unprocessed foods apart from an occasional iced tea sweetened with the sugar substitute Splenda. "There's a hell of a lot of packaged real food out there." He suggests looking for minimally processed options that make cooking faster, such as a salad mix or chopped vegetables.

We have to do our best to make healthy choices, Gearhardt says, but everything is stacked against us. As a food scientist, even she leaves the grocery store befuddled. "It's easy to say we should just tell the individual to do better, [but] everything in the environment is set up for the industry to profit," she says.

In an ideal world, we would focus on making healthy alternatives convenient and affordable and reducing marketing to kids, Gearhardt says. "We need to take some courageous action and have some common sense that this food environment is not good for anybody," she adds.

About the Author

Lori Youmshajekian is a freelance science journalist who reports on advances in health, environmental issues and scientific misconduct. She holds a master's degree in science journalism from New York University and has written for New Scientist, Yale Environment 360, *Retraction Watch and Medscape, among other outlets.*

How Much Caffeine Is Too Much?

By Joanna Thompson

In the land of venti pumpkin spice lattes and caramel macchiatos, Americans frequently partake in caffeine fixes. In fact, most people in the U.S. consume caffeine daily, primarily in the form of coffee, tea and energy drinks. But is there such a thing as too much caffeine?

The U.S. Food and Drug Administration recommends that people consume no more than about five milligrams of caffeine per kilogram (2.2 pounds) of body weight daily, which adds up to around 400 mg for a 79-kg (175-pound) person. Although you may be able to have more without negative consequences, there is theoretically a limit to how much caffeine your body can handle. "You can certainly die from caffeine overdose," says Jose Antonio, a sports and exercise scientist at Nova Southeastern University. Fortunately, consuming that much caffeine is really, really difficult. "We're talking multigram doses," in the neighborhood of 10 grams or more, he says. On average, an eight-ounce (about 240-milliliter) cup of drip coffee prepared at home contains around 100 mg of caffeine, so most people would need to consume more than 100 cups of joe in a single sitting before they started to get into dangerous territory.

The amount of caffeine in a cup of commercially brewed coffee can vary wildly, however. A Starbucks grande dark roast contains about 260 mg of caffeine, while a medium hot coffee from Dunkin' has 210 mg. And some energy drinks can contain up to 300 mg in a 16-ounce (473-milliliter) can. Caffeine pills and powders can be dangerous if taken in bulk and should be used cautiously.

Caffeine, a central nervous system stimulant, blocks the effects of sleep-inducing chemicals, such as adenosine, in your brain. In your bloodstream, it also boosts the circulation of cortisol and adrenaline, both of which cause your heart to beat faster and your energy levels to peak. When a person consumes too much of this stimulant, they can start to feel jittery or overly excitable and may have difficulty sleeping.

Some rare health conditions can make consuming caffeine riskier. Long QT syndrome (LQTS) is a genetic condition named for the lag that it produces in the heart's electrical activity as graphed by an electrocardiogram (ECG). It affects about one in 2,000 people. Under certain circumstances, a sudden jolt of adrenaline might cause someone with LQTS to go into cardiac arrest. "A classic example is someone diving into a swimming pool and suddenly [losing consciousness]," says Gregory Marcus, a cardiologist at the University of California, San Francisco. Because caffeine can cause a similar spike in adrenaline in the bloodstream, individuals with long QT syndrome might need to be careful about their caffeine consumption

In September 2022 a college student with LQTS ordered a "charged lemonade" from the chain restaurant Panera Bread. That product contains between 260 and 390 mg of added caffeine, according to the company. After drinking the beverage, she went into cardiac arrest and died. In October 2023 her family filed a lawsuit against Panera for failing to adequately disclose the drink's caffeine content. The company has since enhanced its caffeine labeling "out of an abundance of caution," said a Panera spokesperson in a statement to NBC News. Marcus says this type of situation is exceedingly rare, however.

Caffeine is addictive but not in the way that comes to mind when people think about most substance use disorders. "Someone can be physically dependent on caffeine and not have what we consider problematic use," says Laura Juliano, a psychologist at American University, who studies caffeine use, among other topics. But if you decide to wean yourself off caffeine, you may want to do it gradually. Withdrawal symptoms can include headache, fatigue, inability to concentrate and occasionally flulike body aches. These symptoms are usually mild, although they can be more severe for some individuals. "I have heard many stories from people who thought they were sick, but it turned out to be caffeine withdrawal," Juliano says.

The American College of Obstetricians and Gynecologists recommends that pregnant people limit their caffeine consumption to about 200 mg (about two home-brewed cups of coffee) a day or less. Too much caffeine might also trigger panic attacks in people with anxiety. Some people might choose to limit their intake for this reason. The exact dose for inducing jitters varies, however, depending on a person's caffeine sensitivity and current stress level. There is a genetic component to caffeine tolerance—in particular, a gene called CYP1A2 determines how fast (and how thoroughly) a person's body metabolizes the drug. People with the "slow" variant of the gene are considered more sensitive to caffeine's effects.

For most people, though, caffeine is safe in moderation. And it can even be beneficial. Contrary to popular belief, Marcus says, there is some evidence that people who use caffeine daily may have a lower risk of arrhythmias, or irregular heart rhythms that can lead to cardiac arrest. Based on his research, people who consume it tend to be more active, taking approximately 1,000 additional steps per day, on average, compared with nonusers. A large body of research has also demonstrated that caffeine can improve athletic performance. Other studies suggest that drinking coffee could reduce the risk of mouth or throat cancer, though this may or may not be a direct result of the caffeine.

So unless you're avoiding caffeine for a specific health, religious or other personal reason, go ahead and enjoy your lattes.

About the Author

Joanna Thompson is an insect enthusiast and former Scientific American intern. She is based in New York City. Follow Thompson on Twitter @jojofoshosho0.

Eating Disorders Can Strike Anyone

By Ashley Andreou

I still don't trust my parents' ability to feed me," confessed Sofia after I asked what she was most anxious about, nearing discharge after two months on an inpatient eating disorders unit where I worked as a psychiatry resident. The 14-year-old girl was brought to the pediatrician by her parents, worried about her eating. They learned that Sofia (whose name has been changed for her privacy) had lost 30 pounds over three months—she was eating only one piece of fruit a day in the weeks leading up to her admission. She could barely walk home from school, her menses ceased, her hair fell out in clumps, and her heart rate dangerously slowed.

But Sofia was not the patient that people often envision with an eating disorder. Her family was Spanish-speaking and had emigrated from Peru. Her confession contained both her fears about losing control of her eating as well as real concern for her life after leaving the hospital.

Her deeply caring family struggled with family sessions during her inpatient treatment, complicated by the need for interpreters, a prescribed inpatient diet that differed from the meals typically eaten at home, and a hesitancy to ask questions of the health care team. While Sofia was successfully restored to a healthy weight at discharge from the hospital, finding appropriate outpatient treatment presented yet another challenge. Family-based treatment is a standardized outpatient therapy, which aims to restore adolescent patients to a healthy weight with the support of their parents; the therapy consists of three phases where the parents begin with most of the feeding responsibility, and the patient gradually gains more autonomy as they become renourished. It is the gold standard for adolescent outpatient therapy. However, Medicaid did not fully cover most of these programs, and finding one with a Spanish-speaking therapist was even rarer. Despite a social worker's efforts, Sofia was wait-listed for a family treatment program with a Spanish-speaking provider who offered sliding-scale payment.

Sofia's case highlights the disconnect between who develops an eating disorder and the stereotypes portrayed in popular TV shows and movies like *13 Reasons Why* and *Black Swan*. Media-fueled misconceptions about eating disorders predominantly affecting white, affluent, young females have resulted in disparities: underdiagnosis, lack of treatment access and limited understanding of eating disorders, leading to poorer outcomes.

Eating disorders include anorexia nervosa, bulimia nervosa, binge-eating disorder and avoidant/restrictive food intake disorder. These diseases have grave physical consequences, such as heart arrhythmias, and psychiatric ones, such as depression and suicidality. They are also on the rise, likely related to social isolation in the wake of the COVID-19 pandemic and increased social media use. With a 5 percent mortality rate, anorexia nervosa is one of the deadliest psychiatric illnesses in the world. From Taylor Swift to Princess Diana to Jane Fonda, eating disorders are not a new phenomenon.

Despite what people may think, eating disorders are equally prevalent across socioeconomic status, racial and ethnic groups, affecting approximately 9 percent of females and 4 percent of males. Emerging data even suggest individuals with multiple marginalized identities may be at higher risk. In one study of over 120,000 people, lower-income individuals were 27 percent more likely to have an eating disorder compared with those of higher income. This research also found that 52 percent of bisexual men and 52 percent of lesbian women of Latinx ethnicity and lower socioeconomic status screened positive for an eating disorder.

Our relationship to food is complex. Likewise, ethnicity, the stress of cultural assimilation, Western beauty standards, racial discrimination and trauma shape the prevalence of eating disorders.

Low-income patients and patients of color are also more likely to have missed diagnoses and not receive treatment. In a statewide study of California's Medicaid-insured youth, the annual eating disorder prevalence was 0.2 percent compared with the 5 percent national prevalence estimate. That highlights the stark underdiagnosis and limited public funding of treatment for eating disorders. Moreover, when compared with national prevalence rates of eating disorders, health care professionals missed around 50 percent of diagnoses in Black youth in the U.S. Diagnostic bias likely underpins this underdiagnosis: presented with identical eating disorder symptoms, clinicians are more likely to diagnose a white patient than a Black patient. Diagnosis and treatment are inextricably linked; correctly identifying patients is the first step in effective treatment. Additionally, training non–mental health care providers in eating disorders is critical; if pediatricians or social workers don't know the warning signs, they won't see them.

Like accurate diagnosis, health care access determines treatment. In the U.S. treatment access is inextricably linked to how much money you have, where you live, who holds political office, stigma and blatant discrimination. One study published in 2018 found that Latinx youth with eating disorders were less likely to use mental health services compared to non-Latinx youth. Affluence was directly correlated with understanding a need for treatment (52 percent more likely) and receiving treatment (89 percent more likely) compared with low-income students in the study. Altogether, specialist services appear less accessible to low-income patients. For instance, eating disorder specialty services concentrate in more affluent areas and many offer services only to those with private health care. Outpatient behavioral health services often deny patients on Medicaid, as shown by Sofia's inability to access family-based treatment. Given these diagnostic and treatment inequities, disparities in disease outcomes are inevitable. Early diagnosis and treatment are the best indicators of recovery and decreases in illness and death.

So how can we change these disparities? Fundamentally, we can't know what we don't study. The lack of inclusive research sustains stereotypes and fuels diagnostic bias. In the majority of eating disorder research, information on socioeconomic status is inconsistent and sexual orientation is absent. Although more studies report race and ethnicity data, funding and recruitment are often limiting factors. There is a seismic difference between collecting data and finding ways to proactively recruit diverse, representative participants. Most people included in eating disorder research are still white women. Few men, people of color, and even fewer gender-diverse individuals have been studied.

Ultimately, diversifying research will enable better treatment. In health care, increased evidence justifies increased investment, a bootstrap effect that helps explain why eating disorder treatment remains desperately underfunded. The heightened risk of patients with multiple minority identities necessitates investigation, including how the intersectional experience of having multiple identities and facing discrimination may affect the disease.

I am thankful that the institution where I work provides full weight restoration treatment at no cost and doesn't need to rely on insurance companies, which would have likely resulted in Sofia being discharged at a much lower weight to outpatient care. However, free specialty care is a rare occurrence in the U.S. And even with quality inpatient treatment, I wish I had more outpatient treatment options to offer Sofia, and couldn't help feeling like the system and we, as an extension of the system, were failing her on discharge. Eating disorders can affect anyone, and changing the narrative is critical in the endeavor for more equitable treatment. To ensure equal treatment for people like Sofia, we must raise awareness about the spectrum of individuals affected by eating disorders and address these biases in research, funding and patient care.

This is an opinion and analysis article, and the views expressed by the author or authors are not necessarily those of Scientific American.

About the Author

Ashley Andreou is a psychiatry resident at New York-Presbyterian/Columbia University Irving Medical Center.

Food Can Be Literally Addictive, New Evidence Suggests

By Marta Zaraska

G iven the option, most rats will choose sugar instead of cocaine. Their lust for the carbohydrate is so intense that they will go as far as to self-administer electric shocks in their desperation to consume sugar. Rats aren't alone in this drive. Humans, it seems, do something similar. People who've had bariatric surgery sometimes continue to overindulge in highly processed foods, those made from white flour, sugar, butter, and the like, even if it means later enduring vomiting and diarrhea. Daily snacking on processed foods, recent studies show, rewires the brain's reward circuits. Cravings for tasty meals light up the brain just like cravings for cocaine do, prompting some researchers to ask whether products such as fries or cookies can trigger addiction akin to that associated with drugs or alcohol.

Yet the issue is by no means settled. An ongoing debate persists over whether these foods are truly addictive. Processed foods might provoke compulsive behaviors that reinforce the need to consume more, but do they really have mood-altering effects, another criterion used to define an addiction?

Answers to these questions are complicated by the enormous variety of foods we consume. There is no single opiatelike substance that can be identified as leading someone to become a food addict. Arguments in favor of food addiction suggest that if carbohydrates and fats are mixed together in unnaturally large doses, this creates a rapid "delivery system" for nutrients that results in physiological effects on the brain's reward system that resemble those produced by cocaine or nicotine.

To examine how this affects actual behaviors, researchers developed a measurement to examine the strong pull that highly processed food exerts on humans.In 2009 the Yale Food Addiction Scale emerged. It is used to assess whether a person displays behavioral patterns that would merit fries, shakes and other palatable foods being classified as addictive substances.

Using this measurement technique, a 2022 meta-analysis suggested that 20 percent of adults are addicted to food. People in this group go out of their way to obtain their favorite foods and often eat to the point of feeling physically ill. They experience withdrawal, fail to quit eating certain foods and continue their consumption pattern despite adverse consequences, such as disruptions to their daily routines and social activities. These are all criteria set out by the Yale Food Addiction Scale, which is adapted from measures used to gauge substance use disorders. The definition of food addiction is separable from obesity. Surprisingly, many people who tick the boxes for food addiction maintain a typical weight. If anything, food addiction is the closest cousin to binge eating disorder, says Alexandra DiFeliceantonio, a neuroscientist at the Fralin Biomedical Research Institute at Virginia Tech Carilion. Both cause people to exhibit a lack of control in the way food is consumed, but the definition for a substance use disorder also includes cravings, withdrawal symptoms and continued use despite negative consequences.

Critics of this research suggest that you can't get addicted to something that's essential to life. What's more, while science has pinpointed nicotine in cigarettes and ethanol in wine or beer as the substances responsible for keeping people hooked, no such clear-cut equivalent exists for food. "It's very difficult to prove that there are these nutrients in food that directly cause addiction," says Johannes Hebebrand, a psychiatrist at the University of Duisburg-Essen in Germany.

Yet Ashley Gearhardt, a clinical psychologist at the University of Michigan, argues that highly processed foods are vastly different from what our ancestors used to consume. "Foods that are very high in fat and carbohydrate in a kind of an equal ratio—they don't exist naturally," she says. "It's something that's designed by food scientists in a laboratory to look a certain way, feel a certain way in your mouth, smell a certain way when you open the package." A 2021 study showed, for example, that people with binge eating disorder exclusively overeat ultraprocessed foods. "People aren't losing control over beans," Gearhardt says.

Early research on rats suggested that sucrose keeps animals hooked. "They want more and more and more. Each day, they'll show signs of craving," says Nicole Avena, a neuroscientist at the Icahn School of Medicine at Mount Sinai. Sugars are present in many natural foods, from bananas to beets. Yet, as Avena points out, it's all about packaging. A piece of fruit, she says, "has the appropriate amount of sugar in it, based on how much fiber it contains. Also, it has other nutrients that are going to minimize or mitigate the effects that that sugar might have on our brain."

What matters, the scientists argue, is the dosage and the speed of absorption of a substance. Most people don't consume pure ethanol, for example. Instead they opt for wine or beer, which contain a small amount of the addictive substance. (Most beer is more than 90 percent water.) Similarly, few of us indulge in sucrose by the spoonful. Nicotine also mixes with other ingredients and is carefully dosed. It's naturally present in eggplants and tomatoes, but you won't become an addict by indulging in vegetables.

When it comes to ultraprocessed snacks, sugar often goes together with fat—a combination that could make such foods even more addictive. A 2018 study by DiFeliceantonio and her colleagues showed that, compared with equally caloric foods containing only fat or only a carbohydrate, those made with both ingredients are far more efficient at activating the striatum, a part of the brain's reward center that is implicated in addictions.

For a 2023 study, DiFeliceantonio and her colleagues randomly assigned 82 people to snack on either high-fat, high-sugar yogurts or low-sugar, low-fat ones for eight weeks. The scientists discovered not only that the first group's preference for the healthier yogurts decreased after the trial but that their brain activation patterns changed, too. When they tasted fatty, sugary milkshakes, those who had been indulging in high-fat, high-sugar snacks had an increased response in their reward circuits, including the striatum.

"Ultraprocessed foods are hijacking the brain in a way you'd see with addiction to drugs," Avena says.

One of the hallmarks of drug addiction, she says, is the release of dopamine in the brain's reward regions. The potency of a fatty, sugary treat in triggering this release was highlighted by a 2023 study in which scientists used positron-emission tomography on a small sample of volunteers. The results showed that indulging in a milkshake leads to a significant release of dopamine in healthy people that can be about one third of what is usually seen with amphetamines—a group of highly addictive stimulant drugs, such as "speed."

The addictive potential of ultraprocessed foods may not relate just to dopamine, however. A 2023 study revealed the importance of the cannabinoid receptor 2 (CB2) in getting hooked on certain foods (in this particular case, chocolate-flavored pellets, because the subjects were mice). Rodents lacking these receptors in the brain are not only less likely to become addicted to cocaine or alcohol, the research showed, but also less prone to food addiction—a finding that may open new paths for treatment of binge eating.

Research on weight-loss drugs provides further evidence that overeating and substance misuse may share common brain processes. Semaglutide (sold under the brand names Ozempic and Wegovy) induces weight loss by mimicking the insulin-increasing gut hormone glucagonlike peptide-1 (GLP-1), and it could potentially aid those struggling with various addictions, too. Animal experiments suggest, for example, that it can reduce dependence on cocaine and opioids. "That supports the argument that foods and drugs, in many ways, can act on the same brain systems," Avena says.

What's more, both illegal drugs and processed foods can induce cravings in the same reward areas of the brain—as demonstrated by a 2023 functional magnetic resonance imaging (fMRI) study. When researchers showed pictures of cocaine to drug addicts or photographs of donuts to healthy people, the same brain regions—ranging from the ventral striatum and amygdala to the cerebellum—lit up in both groups. And the stronger the volunteers' reported craving was, the more intense their neural response was as well.

Withdrawal symptoms, another classic feature of addiction, also seem to be present in connection with ultraprocessed foods. While it's unlikely that anyone experiences physical shakes from quitting cookies, parents who attempt to restrict their children's intake of sugar-sweetened drinks have reported symptoms such as headaches, irritability and social withdrawal in their kids. Similarly, adolescents instructed to abstain from their high intake of sodas for three days complained of decreased motivation and ability to concentrate—along with increased headaches.

Critics of the idea that certain foods may be addictive point out that treats such as burgers don't induce the same kind of "high" that one might experience with opioids or alcohol. "This is totally missing in all the food addiction stories," Hebebrand says. For her part, Gearhardt is not convinced. "By that principle, cigarettes are not addictive, right? You can drive your car while you smoke cigarettes. You can watch your children while you smoke cigarettes," she says. She points to studies indicating that chocolate does have a psychoactive effect and can induce feelings of euphoria at least as much as intravenous nicotine given to smokers can.

In 2022 Gearhardt and DiFeliceantonio published an opinion piece in the journal *Addiction* arguing that highly processed foods should be classified as addictive based on a 1988 Surgeon General report on tobacco products. That document outlined scientific evidence behind cigarettes' addictive nature, including their psychoactive effects and potential to trigger compulsive use. Similar evidence, the scientists argue, already exists for ultraprocessed foods. "If we apply that same criteria to this specific class of foods, it meets every single checkbox," Gearhardt says.

Hebebrand worries, however, that rushing to classify certain foods as addictive could let the sugar industry off the hook too easily. "They can always say, 'Well, this is a matter of debate; we don't know if it really exists,'" he says. The industry has already sponsored research that argues against the existence of sugar addiction, which, for Gearhardt, suggests that it may be following "the playbook of the tobacco industry." After all, nicotine wasn't a clear-cut candidate for an addictive substance, either: it lacks significant mind-altering effects and is not found in large amounts in foods, and researchers don't know the dosage at which it becomes addictive. As a result, and with the help of the tobacco industry, the addictive nature of tobacco was denied for decades. Considering ultraprocessed foods' detrimental health effects—a 2021 meta-analysis showed such products raise mortality risk by 25 percent—Gearhardt argues that it's better to chance misclassifying ultraprocessed foods as addictive than to fail to label them as such when warranted. "It's cigarettes all over again," she says.

About the Author

Marta Zaraska is a freelance writer based in France and author of Growing Young: How Friendship, Optimism and Kindness Can Help You Live to 100 *(Appetite by Random House, 2020). She wrote "Shrinking Animals" in the June 2018 issue of* Scientific American.

Section 5: How to Live a Healthier Life

Is 'Bed Rotting' Good or Bad for Your Sleep?

By Elana Spivak

T he grueling stretch between New Year's Day and springtime can seem interminable. It's tempting to spend the long, gray months in hibernation mode with a book or your phone while you await brighter days.

Enter "bed rotting," the Internet's new favorite inactive activity. More entertaining than just sleeping in and somehow even less productive than being a couch potato, choosing to bed rot is a popular TikTok mental health trend associated with "reclaiming" time that might otherwise be spent on working, exercising, studying or other "productive" activities. It may mean you opt to stay in bed from sunrise to sunset for perhaps even a whole weekend or more, only leaving it to use the bathroom, get food or retrieve other essentials. Some "rotters" report feeling rejuvenated afterward. One Reddit user claimed three days of staying in bed had given them "the best mental focus ... in about 2 months." The post continues: "I felt as if my body was due for a massive upgrade I had been putting off."

Some who choose to start bed rotting might find this practice restorative. But its ostensible benefits can backfire, mucking up the mind and body's most reliable, natural method of resetting.

Elective bed rotting is yet another purportedly wellness-supporting state of rest and relaxation that was spawned by popular online culture, like its social media sibling "goblin mode," which promotes a similar focus on voluntary inactivity. The overall concept even harks back to the trope of the fashionably sickly Victorian woman laid up in bed with a vague malaise—depictions that also reinforced sexism and marginalized those with disability or chronic illness in the 1800s. Indeed, while this restoration method is a catchy trend with healthy, nondisabled people, those with health conditions or disabilities may need to remain in bed for extended periods of time.

Part of the enduring appeal of lying in bed for people who are otherwise able to be mobile may be that it flouts the pervasive norm that exercise and activity are good for our body and mind, even when they feel like the opposite. Heeding our desire to vegetate may simply feel far easier than working out for a few hours a week, as the World Health Organization recommends. Such a practice is almost always done in the one place we most strongly associate with regular shut-eye, which may interfere the recommended seven to nine hours of nightly sleep for the average adult.

"There's so many problems, when it comes to bed rotting, for sleep," says Fiona Barwick, a clinical associate professor and associate division chief of behavioral sleep medicine at Stanford University School of Medicine.

Bed rotting appears to affect three important elements of sleep health, Barwick says. First, she points to the circadian rhythm, our internal clock that's tuned to light and dark and regulates the sleep-wake cycle. Some people participating in the trend may stay in bed all day, perhaps without catching a glimpse of light except the glow of a screen. Receiving no light early in the day followed by getting copious light toward the evening (by switching on all the lights, for example) can scramble this internal clock, which runs close to a 24-hour cycle in most people.

"Light tends to suppress and delay melatonin," the sleep-inducing hormone released by the pineal gland in our brain, Barwick says. "If you're rotting in bed, and you don't get light until the afternoon, you haven't gotten that circadian morning light signal that sets the timing for your sleep the next night."

Circadian rhythm also helps regulate our sleep drive, the biologically innate need to slumber. Sleep drive builds throughout the day, compounded by activity and exercise. Come nighttime, you should feel ready to snooze. But staying in bed for too long can throw your sleep drive out of whack, pushing back your sleepiness window.

And a day of lying around probably means there's no physical activity to help build sleep drive.

Using your bed as a place to spend time awake also influences the third aspect: sleep cues, a major part of sleep hygiene. These cues are the mental associations you form between sleep and certain times, places (such as your bed) and even sensory inputs such as scents. "Making sure your bed is strongly, clearly associated with sleep and not wakeful activities is one of the evidence-based techniques for better sleep," Barwick says. If you spend a day in bed on TikTok, then "the bed-and-sleep cue will be weak, which will not help sleep."

There is such a thing as spending too much time in bed—and that point arrives relatively quickly. "If you're bed rotting for a day, it's not going to be a big deal," Barwick says. Although most sleep experts don't consider the new trend healthy, Barwick says that she's not too worried about people lying around for one afternoon or day, say, once a month. Periods longer or more frequent, however, may cause some backlash in the form of fatigue, a dysregulated internal clock and higher levels of stress from facing duties we have only temporarily escaped.

Excess time in bed can also weigh on mental health and affect sleep that way, according to Alon Avidan, a professor of clinical neurology at the University of California, Los Angeles. Sleep and psychiatric symptoms have a "bidirectional" relationship, he explains. For example, depression might increase fatigue, but sleeping more to relieve that fatigue may also exacerbate depression symptoms. "We demonstrate that poor sleep can actually worsen depression if you don't get sufficient sleep," he says.

If you're staying in bed just a little too much, Avidan emphasizes the importance of understanding why you feel the need to do so in the first place. For example, staying in bed may not only be helpful but essential to those with a disabling chronic illness like long COVID. The issue may also stem from burnout, a physiological problem that can hamper good sleep and all its benefits, or a nagging issue in your waking life. To snap out of a rut, Avidan advises waking up early in your sleep-wake cycle, no matter when you went to sleep, and basking in some natural light, if possible, for about an hour. If you routinely consume caffeine, make sure you get it in within a few hours of waking so it won't impinge on your sleep drive later. And if you feel sleepy, take a 20-minute power nap in the middle of your day. Barwick adds that spending some aimless time wandering outside could help fulfill the urge to take a break—without putting sleep at risk.

Whether any amount of time spent inactive in bed truly helps you sleep and live better is for you to determine, Barwick says. She suggests asking yourself: "Does bed rotting feel truly restorative? Or does it just feel like you're checking out?"

About the Author

Elana Spivack is a science journalist in New York City who covers reproductive health, food science, and more. Follow her on X @ElanaSpivack.

Learning to Accept Discomfort Could Help You Thrive

By J. David Cresswel

C an you imagine getting a root canal or other major dental procedure without novocaine? A scientist colleague of mine recently told me about a painful exposed nerve in his tooth. Rather than requesting a numbing option from his dentist, he used a "focus in" meditation technique to direct all his attention to his mouth with as much calming equanimity as he could muster. Doing so transformed the pain for a few minutes. Each time the dentist touched the tooth, my colleague felt bubbles of joy, and this feeling lasted until the dentist interrupted by asking, "Why are you smiling?"

A fair question is why anyone would want to be fully aware of intensely negative or painful experiences. But what might sound like a punishing choice—to embrace suffering or distress—may in some instances be helpful. A stream of scientific articles suggests that there are benefits in turning toward discomfort or upsetting emotions with acceptance. In addition, all of us can gain from finding ways to cope with stress and unhappiness—particularly when the circumstances are beyond our control. As a researcher who has studied meditation for more than 20 years, I believe that the cultivation of equanimity, a central element of certain mindfulness-meditation practices, can help.

It's important to first define the idea of turning toward discomfort. I'm not advocating for people to put themselves in dangerous or excruciating positions. But when we push ourselves into challenging or discomfiting situations, much like trainers who push athletes just past their comfort zone to make gains, learning often happens. Indeed, a 2022 study involving more than 2,000 people demonstrated that the participants who were explicitly encouraged to push themselves into awkward, uncomfortable situations across multiple domains—including taking improv classes to boost self-confidence and reading about opposing political viewpoints—later reported the greatest degree of personal growth.

Another study, published in 2023, found that people who can face negative emotions such as sadness and anger in a neutral way are more satisfied, are less anxious and have fewer symptoms of depression than those who judge their negative feelings harshly. That study aligns with a growing consensus in psychology that suggests we can learn powerful lessons about ourselves if we can sit with our emotions and thoughts with an open, curious mind.

My own research indicates that meditation provides an ideal way to practice turning toward discomfort—particularly when it improves one's equanimity. Broadly, mindfulness meditation is a form of mental training that helps people focus on attending to the present moment in an open and receptive way. "Equanimity" refers to a mental attitude of being at peace with the push and pull of experience. In my laboratory at Carnegie Mellon University, we conducted several clinical trials on developing equanimity during mindfulness-meditation training. This approach includes guided meditation exercises such as using a matter-of-fact voice to label uncomfortable sensations in the body and welcoming uncomfortable feelings by saying "yes" aloud each time a sensation is detected.

To gauge the effectiveness of such interventions, we recruited 153 stressed adults in Pittsburgh and offered them a mindfulness-meditation training program with or without training in equanimity. For example, the mindfulness-only group built skills to recognize ongoing experiences, whereas the equanimity group practiced acceptance of those experiences in addition to the basic recognition. Our equanimity training group had much better outcomes on several measures. After just 14 days of training, the participants who learned equanimity skills had significantly lower biological stress responses when asked to deliver a difficult speech and solve math problems in front of experts in white lab coats. The equanimity skills group also had lower blood pressure and hormonal stress levels.

In the days after training, people introduced to equanimity exercises reported significantly higher positive emotions and well-being throughout the day and more meaningful social interactions than participants who received mindfulness training without the equanimity component. It was as though developing an attitude of equanimity had transformed their emotional reactivity to stress, helping them better appreciate and savor daily life's many little positive experiences and making them more curious and open to connecting with others.

We are expanding on this work in several ways, including by developing an app that offers equanimity training on demand. We are also conducting trials with participants who have stress-related gastrointestinal disorders. Meanwhile other scientists are further exploring equanimity's power.

In 2022, for instance, researchers based in Australia published a study examining isolation and psychological distress in 578 people during the COVID pandemic. They found that the degree to which people felt alone during that period predicted their depression, anxiety and stress—but this dynamic could be mediated by equanimity. That is, people who reported higher levels of equanimity (based on how much they agreed or disagreed with statements such as "I experience a sense of mental balance regardless of what is happening in my life") reported less psychological distress even though they were feeling isolated. In other words, equanimity can be protective in a way that prevents feelings of social disconnection from leading to mental distress.

Equanimity can help us weather the inevitable periods of suffering that we all face at some point in our life. Many people are hurting and looking for ways to cope. Our social lives are suffering, too, which prompted the U.S. surgeon general to declare a national advisory last year about our surging epidemic of loneliness.

Without question, there are many important steps we need to take collectively to respond to these challenges—including looking closely at societal structures and choices that contribute to these problems. But we can each build resilience on a personal level by cultivating greater acceptance of our experience—good or bad, painful or pleasant—in the present moment.

This is an opinion and analysis article, and the views expressed by the author or authors are not necessarily those of Scientific American.

About the Author

J. David Creswell is the William Dietrich II Chair Professor of Psychology and Neuroscience at Carnegie Mellon University, and chief of science at Equa Health. His Health and Human Performance Laboratory studies what makes people resilient under stress, the science of mindfulness meditation training, and wellness.

Science-Backed Sleep Tips from 2024 to Help You Snooze Better

By Lauren J. Young

B etween jobs, school, kids, and other physical and mental tolls on our time and energy, we could all use better, more restful sleep. There's no question that good shut-eye is important for our health. Research has linked poor sleep with imbalanced sugar levels and metabolism and with elevated risk of cardiovascular issues and neurological conditions, including dementia. And slumbering bodies are very fickle: sleep quality can be easily thrown off by any number of environmental disturbances or emotional or physical stressors.

We're channeling some of the most helpful science-backed tips and findings that sleep experts have shared with us this year—so hopefully we feel more refreshed and reenergized in 2025.

Short Daytime Naps Sharpen the Mind

If you're feeling sluggish in the middle of the day, a short snooze could be the refresher the brain needs. Growing evidence suggests that daytime power naps can actually give a boost to critical thinking skills, memory, productivity and mood. As Science of Health columnist Lydia Denworth reports, there is a science to napping effectively.

It's best to keep napping sessions 20 to 30 minutes long and before 5 P.M., for those who are regularly awake during daytime hours. That's enough time to get in a cycle of "light sleep," which is easier to wake up in, while avoiding disruptions to regular sleep at night. But note that regularly taking very long naps could be a sign of an underlying health issue.

Staying in Bed All Day, or "Bed Rotting," Can Worsen Sleep

"Bed rotting," or opting to stay in bed for prolonged periods of time, is one of social media's favorite mental health trends. Conditions or disabilities may cause people to remain in bed, but bed rotting is seen as a kind of elective counterculture to "productive" activities—the opposite of working, exercising or studying. People who bed rot often claim that they feel rejuvenated after hours or even days during which they stay in bed, only leaving to go to the bathroom or get food.

But experts say this behavior can throw off the body's internal clock, or circadian rhythm, which controls sleep-wake cycles. This could alter someone's sleep drive (making them feel restless when they should be normally asleep) and sleep cues (making them less likely to associate their bed with sleepy times). To get out of a bed rotting cycle, experts say to first evaluate the reason why you feel the need for that kind of mental recharge. Then try to consistently wake up early in your sleep-wake cycle, no matter what time you went to sleep, and get natural light for an hour upon waking, if possible.

The "Sleepy Girl Mocktail" Reminded Us Magnesium Is Important for Sleep

The "sleepy girl mocktail," a concoction of cherry juice, seltzer and magnesium, was another trend that took off this year. People on TikTok touted that the homemade sip helped them slip into slumber more easily. But evidence that it works is up in the air. That said, one of the ingredients, magnesium, has been shown to play a role in sleep. The mineral can help relax muscles and affect pathways in the brain that stabilize mood and anxiety. Magnesium supplements can be found at local drugstores—but some types can act as a laxative that can disrupt sleep.

Sleeping on the Floor Could Benefit Your Back—Sometimes

People have been sleeping on the floor for centuries—and for some cultures today, it's important to well-being. Some people with certain back ailments also could find floor sleeping particularly helpful.

According to some physiotherapists, lying flat on your back, splayed out like a starfish, or tucking your knees up with your back on the floor helps stretch and take pressure off your back. The firmness of the floor might also give more support than a very soft mattress.

Many experts agree that the practice isn't appropriate for every back condition, however. The flatness of floors could lead to joint stiffness, put more pressure on hips and buttocks or reduce the curved shape of your spine, which can result in back pain.

Sleeping Solo Might Be Better for You—And Your Partner

A 2023 survey found that up to a third of couples in the U.S. got a "sleep divorce," a trend that further caught on this year as more people, including celebrities, shared that they are choosing to sleep separately from partners for a better night's rest.

Some evidence suggests that sleeping alone might be better for some couples. A lot of it has to do with differences in sleep compatibility. Research has shown that people with differing sleep schedules, such as night-shift workers and day-shift workers, can have poor sleep if they share a bed, and sleeping with a heavy snorer is more likely to cause fatigue and daytime sleepiness the next day. Researchers note, though, that there are benefits to co-sleeping—it can provide comfort and emotional support, which can relieve stress.

Remedies for When Anxiety Keeps You Awake

Many people lost sleep over the stress of this year's U.S. presidential election—and some may still be lying awake with anxiety. Any stressful event can disrupt sleep quality, but experts say there are actionable tips people can use:

Before bed, put away screens, and try to avoid doomscrolling, or overconsuming news—stop when you feel informed. If you're feeling amped up or angry, de-escalate before getting into bed. Whether it's practicing meditation, drinking a warm beverage, doing a puzzle or knitting, do an activity that gets you into state of sleepiness first—no matter what time it is. Using a lesson from cognitive behavioral therapy, try to turn negative thoughts into positive ones by focusing on things you're grateful for, says Sally Ibrahim, a sleep physician at the University Hospitals health system in northeastern Ohio.

"If I practice it over and over again, those thoughts will in turn calm me down. It gives me peace and joy," she says. "And those are the kinds of things that help not only our mental health but sleep."

About the Author

Lauren J. Young is an associate editor for health and medicine at Scientific American. *She has edited and written stories that tackle a wide range of subjects, including the COVID pandemic, emerging diseases, evolutionary biology and health inequities. Young has nearly a decade of newsroom and science journalism experience. Before joining* Scientific American *in 2023, she was an associate editor at* Popular Science *and a digital producer at public radio's* Science Friday. *She has appeared as a guest on radio shows, podcasts and stage events. Young has also spoken on panels for the Asian American Journalists Association, American Library Association, NOVA Science Studio and the New York Botanical Garden. Her work has appeared in* Scholastic MATH, School Library Journal, IEEE Spectrum, Atlas Obscura *and* Smithsonian Magazine. *Young studied biology at California Polytechnic State University, San Luis Obispo, before pursuing a master's at New York University's Science, Health & Environmental Reporting Program.*

Exercise Helps Your Brain
as Much as Your Body

By J. David Creswell

L et's start thinking differently about exercise.

Decades of exercise science research show that when people or animals are given a new exercise routine, they get healthier. But when thinking about the benefits of exercise, most people hold a strong body bias; they focus on how regular exercise builds more lean body mass, helps increase their strength and balance, or improves heart health. Exercise matters even more for our brains, it turns out, in ways that are often overlooked.

Here's how we know. Animal exercise studies typically run rats for weeks on running wheels. The animals gleefully run every night, sprinting several miles over the course of an evening. There are wonderful health benefits in these studies of voluntary running—improved muscle tone and cardiovascular health, and many brain benefits too. But in some studies, there's an additional experimental condition where some rats exercise with one crucial difference: it's no longer voluntary exercise. Instead of a freestanding running wheel, rats run on a mechanized wheel that spins, *forcing* the animals to cover the same distance as the voluntary runners.

What happens? When the rats are forced to exercise on a daily basis for several weeks, their bodies become more physically fit, but their brains suffer. Animals regularly forced to exercise have the equivalent of an anxiety disorder, behaving on new tasks in highly anxious and avoidant ways. These animals are more anxious not only compared to the voluntary runners, but also to animals that are not given an opportunity to exercise at all. Yes, forced exercise might be worse than no exercise at all. This work suggests something important about the health benefits of exercise: it is not just about making our muscles work, but what exercise does to our brains. When exercise gives us a sense of control, mastery and joy, our brains become less anxious. If we take that away, by forcing exercise, we can shift it from helpful to harmful.

For us free-ranging humans, there are certainly analogues to this forced running, leaving us feeling like we are in our own rat race: we are forced to run across the airport when late to catch a flight, or we are coerced into doing treadmill tests at the cardiologist's office. But it's more than just feeling forced; studies show that even our everyday attitudes and expectations of exercise shape our health. Studies that manipulate whether exercise is framed as helpful (versus just exercise alone) find that shifting our exercise expectations to be more positive significantly improves mood, and improves some markers of physical health, such as lowering resting blood pressure. Our attitudes toward exercise have even been linked to longevity. For example, the confident belief that one exercises more than others has been associated with greater longevity, an effect that persists even after taking into account actual amount of exercise behavior. But if there is one take-home message from exercise studies in humans, however, it is that exercise significantly improves mental health. A groundbreaking paper out in February looked at hundreds of clinical trials of exercise training for treating major depression. It found that while there are some benefits of taking antidepressant medications, exercise programs such as walking, jogging or dancing had two to three times larger effects on improving mental health.

It's not just our psychology that shapes the benefits of exercise; the broader social context of exercise is important as well. A study in Denmark collected information on average weekly exercise routines in over 8,000 adults, and then looked to see what types of exercise were associated with greater longevity 25 years later. While physical activities such as cycling, swimming, jogging or going to the gym had some longevity benefits (about 2.4 additional years of longevity relative to people in the sample who didn't exercise), it was the social sports that were associated with the biggest longevity gains. Tennis and badminton were associated with over three times the longevity benefit, with over eight additional years of longevity.

When I speak to audiences about this study, I often ask them to predict which forms of physical activity are associated with the biggest longevity benefits. There's usually a heavy body bias; people often pick cycling and jogging as the longevity winners because they are good for our joints or they most rigorously train our cardiovascular systems. We easily forget that exercise is also for our brains, and social connection has all sorts of brain health benefits. Scientific studies of relationships suggest that greater social connectivity is associated with twice the longevity benefit compared to regular physical exercise. But we don't have to pit them against each other; social sports combine the best of both, linking exercise to social connection. And yes, it is important to remember that all forms of physical activity offer opportunities for social connection. The Denmark longevity study also showed that slower (and less vigorous) forms of jogging were associated with bigger longevity benefits, suggesting that we don't always need a heart-pumping workout, but that we might also invite a slow jog *with a friend*. Or maybe a pickleball game.

Modern science reminds us to pay new attention to the old Roman saying, "A sound mind in a sound body." Instead of just asking questions about how exercise affects our bodies, let's also consider questions about how it affects our brains. How can I find a way to take my dreaded exercise routine and turn it into something fun? Under what conditions does my exercise provide a sense of mastery and accomplishment? What kind of exercise helps me feel the most mentally strong and in control? Is exercise giving me ways to nurture important relationships with others?

My lab and others show that the mindsets we bring to the challenges and discomforts of life really matter for shaping our resilience and health. Exercise, when done wisely, can become a welcome discomfort that doesn't just improve the health of our bodies, but also our brains.

This is an opinion and analysis article, and the views expressed by the author or authors are not necessarily those of Scientific American.

About the Author

J. David Creswell is the William Dietrich II Chair Professor of Psychology and Neuroscience at Carnegie Mellon University, and chief of science at Equa Health. His Health and Human Performance Laboratory studies what makes people resilient under stress, the science of mindfulness meditation training, and wellness.

Kids Need More Places to Play, Not Fat Shaming

by The Editors

T he rate of childhood obesity in the U.S. has tripled over the past 50 years. But what this trend means for children's long-term health, and what to do about it (if anything), is not so clear.

The American Academy of Pediatrics (AAP) made waves this year by recommending that doctors put obese kids as young as two years old on intensive, family-oriented lifestyle and behavior plans. It also suggested prescribing weight-loss drugs to children 12 and older and surgery to teens 13 and older. This advice marks a shift from the organization's previous stance of "watch and wait," and it reflects the AAP's belief that obesity is a disease and the group's adoption of a more proactive position on childhood obesity.

Yet the lifestyle programs the AAP recommends are expensive, inaccessible to most children and hard to maintain—and the guidelines acknowledge these barriers. Few weight-loss drugs have been approved for older children, although many are used off-label. They have significant side effects for both kids and adults. And surgery, while becoming more common, has inherent risks and few long-term safety data—it could, for instance, cause nutritional deficits in growing children. Furthermore, it's not clear whether interventions in youngsters help to improve health or merely add to the stigma overweight kids face from a fatphobic society. This stigma can lead to mental health problems and eating disorders.

Rather than fixating on numbers on a scale, the U.S. and countries with similar trends should focus on an underlying truth: we need to invest in more and safer places for children to play where they can move and run around, climb and jump, ride and skate.

Moving more may not prevent a child from becoming overweight, but studies show clearly that it helps both physical and mental health. In 2020 the Centers for Disease Control and Prevention found, unsurprisingly, that kids' sports participation increases with their parents' incomes: about 70 percent of kids whose families earn more than $105,000 a year participate in sports, but only 51 percent of middle-class kids and 31 percent of children at or below the poverty line do. This disparity hurts people of color the most. More than 60 percent of white children, for instance, participate in athletics, but only 42 percent of Black children and 47 percent of Hispanic children do. Experts blame these problems on the privatization of sports—as public investment in school-based athletics dwindles, expensive private leagues have grown, leaving many kids out.

According to the U.S. Department of Health and Human Services' Physical Activity Guidelines for Americans, children between ages six and 17 should get at least an hour of moderate to intense physical activity every day. Yet only 21 to 28 percent of U.S. kids meet this target, two government-sponsored surveys found. The nonprofit Active Healthy Kids Global Alliance evaluates physical activity in American children, and in 2022 the group gave the U.S. a grade of D–.

Why is it so hard to get kids moving? In addition to fewer opportunities at school, researchers cite increased screen time, changing norms around letting kids play outdoors unsupervised, and a lack of safe places for them to play outside the home.

New York City, for example, had 2,067 public playgrounds as of 2019—a "meager" amount for its large population, according to a report from the city comptroller—and inspectors found hazardous equipment at one quarter of them. In Los Angeles in 2015, only 33 percent of youths lived within walking distance of a park, according to the L.A. Neighborhood Land Trust. Lower-income neighborhoods tend to have the fewest public play spaces, despite often having a high population density. And although rural areas have more undeveloped outdoor space, they often lack playgrounds, tracks and exercise facilities.

Kids everywhere need more places to play: trails, skate parks and climbing walls, gardens and ball fields, bike paths and basketball courts. Robust public funding to build and keep up these areas is crucial, but other options such as shared-use agreements can make unused spaces available to the public. Only 10 percent of U.S. schools let people into their playgrounds and schoolyards when school's out, the Trust for Public Land found, and opening up these spaces would give 5.2 million more children access. "Play streets"—residential streets or parking lots that are temporarily closed for activities—are another affordable way to give kids more chances to run around.

These opportunities aren't primarily about changing children's waistlines—they're how we keep childhood healthy and fun.

How Much Do Our Thoughts Shape Our Health?

By Ellen Langer & Peter Aungle

Time heals all wounds, as the saying goes. But any medical professional can tell you that the hours required for recovery after an injury can vary widely. A person's age, lifestyle and level of social support, for example, are all known influences on how quickly their body heals.

Their thoughts can play a remarkably powerful role as well. In a recent experiment, we tested whether expectations about the time it takes to heal can affect how long it actually takes to recover. We found that people's perception of the passage of time influenced how quickly their wounds healed. The work is just the latest in a larger collection of evidence—documented in a new book written by one of us (Langer), *The Mindful Body*—that underscores the unity of mind and body, an idea with profound implications for health and well-being.

For the past 45 years, members of the Langer Lab have studied the ways in which the mind shapes the physiology of the body, or what our lab refers to as mind-body unity. The basic idea is simple: when people conceive of the mind and the body as a single entity rather than separable units, they can see how the mind has enormous control over health and well-being. Wherever we put our mind, so too will be our body.

The first test of this concept was the counterclockwise experiment, which one of us (Langer) designed and ran in 1979. In that study, elderly men lived in a retreat that was retrofitted to appear as if it had existed 20 years earlier and had vintage furniture, appliances and magazines. We asked the men to live as their younger self. They discussed past events in the present tense as if they were currently unfolding. The results were astonishing. Without any medical intervention, their hearing, vision, memory and strength improved. They also were perceived to look noticeably younger in photographs by the end of the week.

Since that time the Langer Lab has found further confirmation of mind-body unity. We have discovered that expecting fatigue can cause people to feel more tired and that thinking you will catch a cold is associated with an increased likelihood of doing so. In another study, people who anticipated certain benefits such as weight loss from daily exercise did see those benefits, even as other people doing the same activities without those expectations saw no such changes.

In the recent study of wound healing, we looked closely at how expectations could affect recovery from a physical injury. We recruited 33 participants to undergo a controlled procedure three times that left mild bruising on the skin. In each case, there was a 28-minute healing observation period, and during that time frame, we asked people to fill out a survey at specific intervals.

In two conditions, we manipulated the experience of time. For example, in a "fast time" condition, we told participants to respond to the survey every eight minutes, and we gave them a timer that—unbeknownst to them—ran at double speed. As a result, every actual minute corresponded to two minutes on the timer, such that the 28-minute total felt like a quick 56 minutes. In a "slow time" condition, the survey occurred every two minutes, and we set the timer to run at half its normal speed. In this setup, the 28-minute period felt like a glacial 14 minutes.

We found that wounds healed faster when participants believed more time had passed and slower when they believed less time had passed—even though the actual elapsed time was the same in every case. We are now in the process of replicating and extending this finding to people recovering from hernia surgery, cataract surgery and dental surgery.

Our implicit beliefs about time are not the only thing we can change to improve our health—our research suggests we should also think more mindfully about categories and diagnostic labels. For example, when we spoke with endocrinologists, they agreed that there was no relevant difference between someone who measured a

5.6 percent or 5.7 percent on a hemoglobin test called A1C, which measures blood sugar levels. But a line must be drawn somewhere, and standard medical protocol is to consider anyone with an A1C level below 5.7 percent as having "normal" levels and anyone above that point as "prediabetic." In a study that was recently accepted for publication, we compared data from 3,984 people who scored a 5.6 percent or 5.7 percent and found a significant difference in their ensuing medical trajectory. Those who got the prediabetic label experienced significantly greater increases in A1C results over the ensuing 10 years and had a significantly higher tendency to develop diabetes. Because the two groups were essentially the same at the start, the most reasonable conclusion is that subsequent differences were the result of the diagnostic label.

While it's worth noting that doctors may have treated these people differently once they received the prediabetic label, many endocrinologists told us that they generally give patients with either a 5.6 or 5.7 percent score the same advice: they note that the patient's blood glucose level is a little high and suggest that lifestyle changes could help. We therefore suspect people with this classification tended to have different expectations for themselves— even though, initially, people in both groups had comparable blood sugar levels on the high side of normal. We dubbed this tendency for otherwise comparable people to fall victim to the diagnostic label they are given "the borderline effect": when we set a threshold for a specific medical condition, people immediately above that borderline and those immediately below it may be essentially the same, but after the label is applied, they leave with very different impressions of their health.

Taken together, this work suggests that people can think themselves sick when they could otherwise be healthy and that they can also think themselves well. Each person goes through life acquiring various beliefs about how their body works and what it means to be healthy. Often these ideas reflect our core assumptions about the world and affect us with little conscious awareness. Much as someone can develop preferences or biases based on past experience, our research suggests that people also develop implicit beliefs that affect their health. For instance, a person may think they can spot the signs that they are getting sick or older. Their expectations, which structure how they feel, what they think and what they do, shape what happens next.

Going a step further, healthy living, which is undoubtedly a function of healthy choices, such as wearing sunscreen and brushing our teeth, is *also* a function of healthy thinking. As one of us (Langer) has argued for decades, most people act mindlessly most of the time because they are preoccupied with their past thoughts, which blinds them to the present. But we can notice and question our thoughts and implicit beliefs, especially when they're counterproductive—such as expecting to heal slowly or thinking we are just too frail to cope.

We can ask ourselves questions such as: How do we know that these ideas are accurate? What past experiences and situational factors might be unduly influencing our beliefs? Are there equally valid alternative beliefs to consider? And when we encounter a more constructive alternative that resonates, we can embrace it. Thoughts, feelings, and actions will then change accordingly. Just like that, better health is often only a thought away.

This is an opinion and analysis article, and the views expressed by the author or authors are not necessarily those of Scientific American.

About the Authors

Ellen Langer is a professor of psychology at Harvard University who has earned three distinguished scientist awards and a Liberty Science Center Genius Award. Her most recent book, The Mindful Body: Thinking Our Way to Chronic Health, *presents, among other things, several studies on mind-body unity and its potential to improve health and well-being.*

Peter Aungle is a Ph.D. candidate in psychology at Harvard University. He is leading investigations into wound healing and the borderline effect. Peter's research explores the ways in which attention, beliefs and expectations interact to shape health over time.

The Biggest Health and Medicine Stories of 2023

By Tanya Lewis

I n a world with so much urgent and depressing news, it can be hard to take a moment and reflect on all of the encouraging scientific and medical progress that has happened. But looking back at 2023, there was plenty on the health beat to be awed by.

From the arrival of the first safe and effective vaccines for a common respiratory disease to the first U.S. Food and Drug Administration–approved CRISPR gene editing treatment, these were some of the biggest stories in the health world this year.

New Weight-Loss Drugs Revealed New Tricks

A new generation of drugs that result in significant weight loss appeared on the scene a few years ago with dramatic effects. This past year we learned a lot more about other potential benefits of the drugs, which include Novo Nordisk's Wegovy and Ozempic and Eli Lilly's Mounjaro. These range from reducing the risk of heart attack or stroke to possibly treating addiction. But the medications come with side effects such as gastrointestinal problems and muscle loss. They're not cheap, either—they can cost around $1,000 or more out of pocket—and it's not clear whether insurance will cover them. Still, these drugs are driving significant interest as we continue to learn more about them.

The COVID Public Health Emergency Ended

The federal public health emergency put in place to combat the COVID pandemic ended on May 11. The end of the public health emergency marked the conclusion of a set of policies that made it easier and cheaper to access COVID tests, vaccines and treatments, as well as telehealth visits. Consumers must now obtain many of these things with coverage through private insurance, Medicare, or Medicaid or bear the cost themselves. SARS-CoV-2, the virus that causes COVID, continues to circulate and pose a threat to public health. But in May the World Health Organization declared that disease no longer constituted a public health emergency of international concern and said that it was time to transition to long-term management of the COVID pandemic.

We Got Closer to Xenotransplants

There's an enormous need for organ transplants, but donor organs are in short supply. Improvements in transplant science have made more organs available and usable. Yet too many people still die waiting for one. Now some scientists are exploring another approach: transplanting organs from nonhuman animals. In the past year they have made significant progress in such "xenotransplants." Following the first transplant of a genetically engineered pig heart into a human in early 2022, this year doctors completed the second such transplant. (Both surgeries were performed on a compassionate use basis because the recipients were terminally ill.) Sadly, the man who received the heart in the latest surgery died after six weeks, likely because his immune system rejected the organ. Other researchers completed successful xenotransplant experiments in people who had suffered brain death, and monkeys that received pig kidneys survived for up to two years. Scientists are hopeful that they can improve the procedures enough to test these techniques in clinical trials in people soon.

RSV Vaccines Finally Arrived

Respiratory syncytial virus (RSV) causes annoying coldlike symptoms in most people, yet in very young children or older adults the disease can be deadly. For decades scientists have tried to develop a vaccine to protect against RSV, but a series of disastrous clinical trials in the 1960s ended up making the illness more severe, leading to the deaths of two children. Researchers persisted, however, and as of this year, several safe and effective RSV vaccines were approved by the FDA to protect pregnant people and older adults. The agency also approved an antibody drug that protects children after they're born.

The First CRISPR-Based Treatment Was Approved

Nearly a decade after it was first discovered, the gene editing method known as CRISPR is resulting in its first treatments. In December the FDA approved the first CRISPR-based treatment for sickle cell disease. The new therapy is known as exa-cel and made by the biotech companies Vertex Pharmaceuticals and CRISPR Therapeutics. It deactivates a faulty gene for the hemoglobin protein, which transports oxygen around the body. Without the treatment, the gene causes blood cells to develop a sicklelike shape, making them clog up blood vessels. The illness, which disproportionately affects Black people, causes debilitating pain and fatigue. The new treatment, as well as another gene therapy approved at the same time, prevented symptoms of the disease for a year in clinical trials. But longer follow-up is needed to see if there are any side effects, and the cost could make it hard for many people to access.

We Gained New Insight into Long COVID

Even as the immediate danger of COVID has receded somewhat, tens of millions of people continue to be affected by long COVID—a cluster of symptoms such as fatigue, body aches and brain fog that linger long after an infection. The causes of long COVID are still mysterious, yet as Stephani Sutherland wrote in our March issue, it increasingly resembles a neurological disease. Not only does it cause cognitive problems with memory, attention, sleep and mood, but it also has symptoms such as pain and postexertional malaise—extreme fatigue after exercise—that seem to stem from the autonomic nervous system, the autopilot system that controls breathing and digestion, among other things. This new understanding could help guide treatments.

Chat-Based AI Systems Entered Medicine

When ChatGPT was released in November 2022, it caused ripples throughout numerous fields—and medicine was no exception. This chat-based artificial intelligence program made by the company OpenAI—along with large language models made by Google and others—is capable of generating text that convincingly mimics human writing. People have already begun to use these programs to diagnose medical conditions, and while the AIs appear surprisingly accurate in some early studies, doctors caution that they are not a substitute for professional medical care. Other people are turning to AI chatbots for therapy. Such apps could help meet the growing demand for mental health services, but as with using them for medical advice, experts urge caution.

First Face and Eye Transplant Was Completed

Xenotransplants weren't the only groundbreaking type of transplant to occur this year. In May doctors in New York City completed the first partial face and whole-eye transplant in an Arkansas man who had suffered severe electrical burns while working as a lineman. While corneal transplants are routine, this was the first time an entire human eye was transplanted and remained healthy six months later, according to the transplant team. The recipient, 46-year-old Aaron James, has not regained sight in that eye, but doctors say the eye's retinal tissue is intact, and there are signs it may be sending signals to the brain. The feat opens the door to restoring the appearance—and possibly, one day, the function—of people who have had traumatic eye injuries.

About the Author

Tanya Lewis is a senior editor covering health and medicine at Scientific American. *She writes and edits stories for the website and print magazine on topics ranging from COVID to organ transplants. She also appears on* Scientific American's *podcast* Science, Quickly *and writes* Scientific American's *weekly Health & Biology newsletter. She has held a number of positions over her eight years at* Scientific American, *including health editor, assistant news editor and associate editor at* Scientific American Mind. *Previously, she has written for outlets that include* Insider, Wired, Science News, *and others. She has a degree in biomedical engineering from Brown University and one in science communication from the University of California, Santa Cruz. Follow her on Bluesky @tanyalewis.bsky.social.*

GLOSSARY

a priori Relating to or denoting reasoning or knowledge which proceeds from theoretical deduction rather than from observation or experience.

anthropogenic Environmental changes that are caused or processed by humanity.

cortisol A hormone produced by the adrenal cortex and used to respond to stress.

doldrums A state or period of inactivity, stagnation, or depression.

epidemic A widespread occurrence of an infectious disease in a community at a particular time.

epidemiologist A scientist who monitors infectious diseases, bioterrorism threats, and other problem areas for public health agencies.

equanimity Mental calmness, composure, and evenness of temper, especially in a difficult situation.

exacerbate To make a problem, bad situation, or negative feeling worse.

immunocompetence Having a normal immune response.

longevity A long life.

meta-analysis An examination of data from a number of independent studies of the same subject, in order to determine overall trends.

multifaceted Containing multiple sides (physical) or containing multiple features (ideological).

paradigm A typical example or pattern of something; a model.

pathogens Bacteria, viruses, or other microorganisms that can cause disease.

psychosis A severe mental condition in which thought and emotions are so affected that contact is lost with external reality.

pulmonologist A physician who specializes in the respiratory system.

transient Lasting only for a short time; impermanent.

ubiquitous Present, appearing, or found everywhere.

FURTHER INFORMATION

Denworth, Lydia. "The Kids (Who Use Tech) Seem to Be All Right." *Scientific American*, January 15, 2019. www.scientificamerican.com/article/the-kids-who-use-tech-seem-to-be-all-right.

Hall, Shannon. "Long COVID Rates Appear to Be Decreasing." *Scientific American*, December 1, 2023. www.scientificamerican.com/article/long-covid-rates-appear-to-be-decreasing.

Lewis, Tanya. "People, Not Science, Decide When a Pandemic Is Over." *Scientific American*, March 14, 2022. www.scientificamerican.com/article/people-not-science-decide-when-a-pandemic-is-over1.

Myers, Katie, Zoya Teirnstein & Grist. "As Hurricane Floodwaters Recede, a Public Health Threat Rises." *Scientific American*, October 22, 2024. www.scientificamerican.com/article/as-hurricane-floodwaters-recede-a-public-health-threat-rises.

Obradovic, Nick, Robin Migliorini, Martin P. Paulus, and Iyad Rahwan. "Empirical Evidence of Mental Health Risks Posed by Climate Change." PNAS, October 8, 2018. www.pnas.org/doi/10.1073/pnas.1801528115.

Pappas, Stephanie. "5 Things We've Learned from COVID in Three Years." *Scientific American,* March 13, 2023. www.scientificamerican.com/article/lessons-learned-after-three-years-of-the-covid-pandemic.

Young, Lauren J. "How to Protect Yourself from Smoky Wildfire Air." *Scientific American*, June 7, 2023. www.scientificamerican.com/article/how-to-protect-yourself-from-smoky-wildfire-air1.

CITATIONS

1.1 Why Some People Get Sick More Often by Elana Spivack (June 21, 2023); 1.2 Confronting the Dangers of Silent Spread Is Necessary to Prevent Future Pandemics by Joshua S. Weitz (November 25, 2024); 1.3 How Risky Are Repeat COVID Infections? What We Know So Far by Meghan Bartles (February 13, 2024); 1.4 COVID Rates Are Rising Again. Why Does It Spread So Well in the Summer? By Tanya Lewis (July 16, 2024); 1.5 Long COVID Is Harming Too Many Kids by Blake Murdoch (October 18, 2024); 1.6 Vaccination Dramatically Lowers Long COVID Risk by Shannon Hall (January 3, 2024); 1.7 Masks Work. Distorting Science to Dispute the Evidence Doesn't by Matthew Oiver, Mark Ungrin & Joe Vipond (May 5, 2023); 2.1 COVID Is Driving a Children's Mental Health Emergency by Julia Hotz (December 13, 2021); 2.2 Social Media Can Harm Kids. Could New Regulations Help? by Jesse Greenspan (May 26, 2023); 2.3 Summertime Sadness Could Be a Type of Seasonal Affective Disorder by Lauren Leffer (July 3, 2024); 2.4 Why Just One Sleepless Night Makes People Emotionally Fragile by Eti Ben Simon (August 15, 2023); 2.5 Losing a Grandparent Hurts Boys at School by Michelle S. Livings, Emily Smith-Greenaway, Rachel Margolis & Ashton M. Verdery (December 18, 2023); 2.6 Aggression Disorders Are Serious, Stigmatized, and Treatable by Abigail Marsh, (February 9, 2024); 3.1 Air Pollution Is Really Dangerous, Even More Evidence Shows by Jesse Greenspan (December 1, 2023); 3.2 Treating Mental Health as Part of Climate Disaster Recovery by Anna Mattson (October 17, 2023); 3.3 Americans Have Breathed More Wildfire Smoke in Eight Months Than in Entire Years by Meghan Bartles (August 15, 2023); 3.4 Wildfires and Smoke Are Harming People's Mental Health. Here's How to Cope by Stephanie Pappas (June 29, 2023); 3.5 How Wildfires Kill People by Tanya Lewis (August 11, 2023); 3.6 Hurricanes Kill People for Years after the Initial Disaster by Andrea Thompson (October 2, 2024); 3.7 What's in Floodwaters? Meghan Bartles (August 30, 2023); 4.1 How a Chemist and His 'Poison Squad' Inspired the First Food Safety Regulations by Tanya Lewis (May 21, 2024); 4.2 The FDA Is Changing What Foods Can Be Called 'Healthy' by Reyna Gobel (December 27, 2024); 4.3 How Do Ultraprocessed Foods Affect Your Health? By Lori Youmshajekian (November 8, 2023); 4.4 How Much Caffeine Is Too Much? By Joanna Thompson (December 1, 2023); 4.5 Eating Disorders Can Strike Anyone by Ashley Andreou (August 15, 2024); 4.6 Food Can Be Literally Addictive, New Evidence Suggests by Marta Zaraska (September 11, 2023); 5.1 Is 'Bed Rotting' Good or Bad for Your Sleep? by Elana Spivak (March 11, 2024); 5.2 Learning to Accept Discomfort Could Help You Thrive by J. David Cresswell (November 10, 2023); 5.3 Science-Backed Sleep Tips from 2024 to Help You Snooze Better by Lauren J. Young (December 13, 2024); 5.4 Exercise Helps Your Brain as Much as Your Body by J. David Creswell (May 1, 2024); 5.5 Kids Need More Places to Play, Not Fat Shaming by The Editors (July 1, 2023); 5.6 How Much Do Our Thoughts Shape Our Health? by Ellen Langer & Peter Aungle (May 3, 2024); 5.7 The Biggest Health and Medicine Stories of 2023 by Tanya Lewis (December 19, 2023).

Each author biography was accurate at the time the article was originally published.

INDEX